Praise for *Leading KidMin*

Pat has led children's ministry at Willow Creek for more than three decades, and Matt has done incredible work through Awana. *Leading KidMin* captures their passion for developing leaders of our most valuable and vulnerable commodity: the kids who will someday lead the church of tomorrow. *Equip your children's team with their wisdom, and soak it up for yourself.* The local church is the hope of the world—and when your children's ministry is thriving, the ripple effect is felt for generations to come.

BILL HYBELS
Senior Pastor, Willow Creek Community Church

In our rapidly and dramatically changing culture, the church is one generation away from death. Children are the future of the church, and also very much today's church, and they are walking away from the church at an alarming rate. Simply hoping that every trendy new program that comes along will keep kids engaged isn't the solution. Kids ministry leaders have the most strategic position in the church, a unique vantage point from which to understand the changes that are needed to serve the church's broader mission. Yet they are often not able to wield the influence necessary to implement that change. What's needed is a major paradigm shift, both within the kidmin leader and within church leadership. Learn from this powerful book how to go from being a director of those who faithfully nurture "the least of these" to also being a church-wide change agent who enables the transformation needed to rescue the future of your church.

WESS STAFFORD
President Emeritus, Compassion International

Some of the most vital work of the church is done in children's ministry. Veteran leaders Pat Cimo and Matt Markins offer practical advice to "kidmin" directors for refining your own perspective on your calling, and working with other ministry partners to make your efforts more effective for the Kingdom.

JIM DALY
President, Focus on the Family

There is no doubt that there is today a most incredible movement of the Holy Spirit in the world of Kid and Family Ministry. As this movement of God continues, what is most needed is strong and effective leadership. This book, by two of America's finest experts in the field, will not only help you refine your leadership skills but it will give you the understanding of how to influence and implement change in helping families succeed. I highly recommend this book.

JIM BURNS
President   *imate Marriage* and
Confident

D1056977

There are amazing leadership books where great principles must be contextualized to your unique ministry situation and there are highly applicable ministry books that offer a "how-to" approach to practical ministry. *Leading KidMin* is one of those rare books that does both! What an excellent new resource for kidmin!

KENNY CONLEY
Leading KidMin Blogger and Influencer; NextGen Pastor, Mission Church, Gilbert, AZ

In children's ministry, it's very easy to get lost in the weeds with so many details to take care of. *Leading KidMin* is a well-needed addition to the ministry leader's toolbox as it challanges you to lead your leaders, and lead yourself, through the prism of the local church rather than cultural trends.

SAM LUCE
Leading KidMin Blogger and Influencer; Pastor of Families, Redeemer Church, Albany, NY

Leading a diverse team inside the local church toward a major paradigm shift is no easy task. It requires someone with great people skills. Add in some sharp, strategic thinking skills—throw in passion, patience, and prayer. Pat Cimo is that kind of leader, and this book lets all of us benefit from her proven practical insights.

SUE MILLER
Orange Volunteer Champion

When I was a young high school student wondering if children's ministry was the path God had called me to, Pat Cimo gave me the opportunity to lead and to be mentored by her. All these years later, she continues to serve as an inspiration and helpful guide for me and so many other church leaders, and I couldn't be more thrilled that together with Matt Markins, they've bundled their expertise into book form so that all now have access to their wisdom.

AMY DOLAN
Family Pastor and Church Consultant, Willow Creek Community Church, Downtown Chicago

As a youth worker for so many years I know the value, and the challenge, of leading up. I'm so thankful for Matt's experience and wisdom helping kids' ministry leaders do just that. You're making a difference in kids' lives, now make a difference in the life of the church.

JOSH GRIFFIN
Cofounder, Download Youth Ministry; Former High School Pastor, Saddleback Church

Pat and Matt have created something as practical as it is insightful. Much has been written about *doing* kidmin well. This book shows you how to *lead* kidmin well. You will be encouraged and challenged to evaluate not only your ministry, but yourself as well! If you want to lead for the long haul . . . read this book!

KEITH FERRIN
Blogger, speaker, and author of *How to Enjoy Reading Your Bible*

Children's ministry is about kids . . . and leadership! If you want to make a significant impact, you must know how to chart a visionary course that volunteers will passionately follow. And charting the course often involves leading through change. I am excited about Matt and Pat's new book. It offers practical steps to help children's ministry leaders guide their ministries to new levels of effectiveness and fruitfulness.

DALE HUDSON
Director of Children's Ministries, Christ Fellowship Church, Palm Beach, FL

I've seen both Pat and Mark in action as leaders. They understand the vital role of children's ministry instilling strong faith in the next generation. We all know that parents are the main influence on a child's spiritual journey. But the church is the main influence on parents. *Leading KidMin* offers seasoned wisdom on how to leverage that influence well. Read and glean!

KURT BRUNER
Author of *It Starts at Home* and host of DriveFaithHome.com

Leading KidMin is a valuable resource for leaders that are interested in developing themselves as leaders first and foremost. In today's current ministry climate where an overemphasis is placed on results, *Leading KidMin* leads one back to the often overlooked, singularly important notion that who we are becoming as leaders in Jesus Christ is the key to flourishing ministry. This is a book rich in wisdom that you will find yourself returning to over and over again.

NANCY J. KANE
Associate Professor, Moody Bible Institute

Leading
KidMin

How to Drive *Real Change*
in Children's Ministry

Leading
KidMin

PAT CIMO
MATT MARKINS

MOODY PUBLISHERS

CHICAGO

© 2016 by
PAT CIMO AND MATT MARKINS

Unless otherwise indicated, all Scripture quotations are taken from the *Holy Bible*, New Living Translation, copyright © 1996, 2004, 2015 by Tyndale House Foundation. Used by permission of Tyndale House Publishers, Inc., Carol Stream, Illinois 60188, U.S.A. All rights reserved.

Scripture quotations marked ESV are from The Holy Bible, English Standard Version® (ESV®), copyright © 2001 by Crossway, a publishing ministry of Good News Publishers. Used by permission. All rights reserved.

Edited by Elizabeth Cody Newenhuyse
Interior design: Ragont Design
Cover design: Gilbert & Carlson Design LLC dba Gearbox
Cover image of arrows copyright © Iveta Angelova/Shutterstock (141969478). All rights reserved.

Library of Congress Cataloging-in-Publication Data

Names: Cimo, Pat, author.
Title: Leading KidMin : how to drive real change in children's ministry / Pat Cimo and Matt Markins.
Description: Chicago : Moody Publishers, 2016. | Includes bibliographical references. | Description based on print version record and CIP data provided by publisher; resource not viewed.
Identifiers: LCCN 2016018873 (print) | LCCN 2016015954 (ebook) | ISBN 9780802494610 () | ISBN 9780802414649
Subjects: LCSH: Church work with children.
Classification: LCC BV639.C4 (print) | LCC BV639.C4 C55 2016 (ebook) | DDC
259/.22--dc23
LC record available at https://lccn.loc.gov/2016018873

We hope you enjoy this book from Moody Publishers. Our goal is to provide high-quality, thought-provoking books and products that connect truth to your real needs and challenges. For more information on other books and products written and produced from a biblical perspective, go to www.moodypublishers.com or write to:

Moody Publishers
820 N. La Salle Boulevard
Chicago, IL 60610

1 3 5 7 9 10 8 6 4 2

Printed in the United States of America

To Jenna, Taryn, Dave, and Ellie—the four little grandchildren who have opened the eyes and heart of their Nonni to truly come to Jesus as His little child every time we sing, dance, play hide-and-seek, and laugh together. You have taught me how to see God in every moment we share.

PAT CIMO

To Katie and Ron, you have modeled alongside of me the very essence of leading change as spiritual leaders from within the crucible.

MATT MARKINS

CONTENTS

Foreword

As a researcher (and the father of three daughters), I know the importance of children's ministry. I know that most conversions in most churches take place during those critical children's ministry years. I know that kidmin leaders are both exceedingly important—and often ignored. They're the ones who are most in tune with the changing needs of the family today. They see what is coming—and engage the future that's already here. They get the need for change in how we minister to our kids and families.

However, making those changes happen in a church setting is often a challenge. All of us, including myself, who have been privileged to serve in the local church know *why* change is often needed and what we can do to implement that change. Here, Pat Cimo and Matt Markins, bringing years of experience with significant kid-focused ministries, look at the how of leading change in children's ministry.

Kidmin leaders often look to "programs" to drive change, which is understandable. That's how much of the ministry is done. However, by doing this, they are missing out on deeper, more robust conversations—conversations that drive change on a more systemic level.

Pat and Matt show us how some of these conversations work and how to move toward building partnerships, learning to listen even when it hurts, aligning to the grander vision of the church, knowing, studying, and understanding the lead pastor. Most importantly, they emphasize the need to "lead from within"—to lead with a different posture, seeking to understand your own leadership voice and applying that to the everyday challenges all in children's ministry face. Such an approach will help your voice to be heard, understood and more influential for total church buy-in and ultimately for the Kingdom.

This book will help you lead in such a way that you have the influence you need to lead in kidmin and beyond.

ED STETZER
Professor
Billy Graham Distinguished Chair
Wheaton College

Introduction: A Pathway for Leading Change

Becoming a change agent starts with the heart of a leader . . . it starts with you.

Like you, we—Pat and Matt—love children's ministry. We believe every child is a gift from God. Speaking into their spiritual lives is an honor and a privilege. We love creating an environment where the hunger within a child to know God more fully grows beyond head knowledge into their heart.

But—like you—there are things we don't love about children's ministry. The struggle of navigating between the worlds of church, culture, and trends: for example, do we allow today's culture to define our creativity and content within children's ministry? Do we stand up for consistent attendance from our families, or do we support the busyness in their lives by sending the message that church is an optional experience by how we organize our various activities and events? Which children's ministry trend do we jump on, and how do we share that trend with our leadership?

And so much more. How do we change things?

We start with three Big Thoughts:

1. Don't just follow trends—you need to lead.
2. Make sure your children's ministry is in the flow of where your church is headed.
3. Change yourself first.

These Big Three ideas apply no matter the size of your church or what kind of team you're leading.

Maybe you can relate to what Pat shares:

I absolutely love children's ministry! Like you, I believe every child is a gift from God. Speaking into their spiritual lives is an honor and a privilege. I love creating an environment where the hunger within a child to know God more fully grows beyond head knowledge into their heart. You and I, as kidmin leaders, have the opportunity to bring kids on a journey of learning about, growing in, and living for God.

But, honestly speaking, there are things I don't love about children's ministry. I don't love the internal struggle I feel as a kidmin leader, navigating between the worlds of culture, trends, and church leadership. There have been times when I have felt caught up in a cyclone of questions. Do we allow today's culture to define our creativity and content within children's ministry? Do we stand up for consistent attendance from our families, or do we support the busyness in their lives by sending the message that church is an optional experience by how we organize our various activities and events? Which children's ministry trend do we choose to move into our kidmin that will bring a spiritual revolution and change the game of our ministry? How do we share the vision of the trend with church leadership so they take on some responsibility of moving this trend forward? Or does every kidmin leader need to accept taking on the responsibility of carrying this vision on their shoulders?

At times I found myself living between the tension of longing to lead vs. coordinating the desires of church leadership, which is a tension many kidmin leaders, directors, and volunteers can relate to.

There were many nights I lay awake frustrated, feeling alone in moving our children's ministry forward. I found myself praying, "God, this isn't what I thought it was going to be."

There were even nights I found myself begging God to release me from children's ministry altogether. As dark as those nights were, I can tell you God hears and speaks to His children. God wants to bring us beyond worrying about finding props for the Bible story or the amount of budget we should be spending on our upcoming preschooler Christmas play. He knows how difficult it is to face weekend after weekend without enough volunteers. He hears our frustration with not being told the weekend adult service would go longer than expected.

It was in the quietness of those nights God showed me this was His ministry and He was using it to change me as a leader. I thought I needed to change my ministry, but God needed to change me.

BECOMING A CHANGE AGENT
IS MORE THAN ADOPTING A TREND

The children's ministry trends we discover at conferences and in books are great, but if we rely on these trends to be the game changer (solution) for our ministries, we can find ourselves frustrated over the lack of church leadership, volunteers, and families embracing these trends to the fullest. These will only be embraced as part of the fabric of your church when you and I lead with the heart of being an influential change agent. *Leading KidMin* is about driving the real change in children's ministry that will influence the future of your church. Don't miss out on the leadership journey God has for you. *Becoming a change agent starts with the heart of a leader . . . it starts with you.*

We, Pat and Matt, have over forty years of experience in children's ministry combined. We've been there. We've based this book on best practices, solid research, and a lot of real ministry experience. We share stories and wisdom learned along the journey of how to move from being a kidmin coordinator to a leader who serves as a change agent—one who has an expanded influence within their church. Each chapter will bring you to a place of internal, or should we say eternal, processing—of coming out the other side different. That separates the change agent leader from the coordinator.

The promise of this book is to give you a clear, practical pathway for leading change, combined with individual and team reflection that will increase your leadership, influence, and overall effectiveness.

Through what means? We have taken ministry and church leadership best practices, qualified research, forty-plus years of real ministry leadership experience, and practical success stories from fellow kidmin leaders that will help you implement change in your kidmin—changes that can lead to total church buy-in.

But why do we need another ministry leadership book? There have been many kids ministry and family ministry books, curricula, and other resources on the need for change (the *why* and the *what*), but very little on *how* to actually lead, influence, and implement change. Matt and I believe that, regardless of the strategy (the *what*), kidmin leaders often struggle with how to actually do all this and what successful implementation would look like in our various ministry settings.

This book is not a how-to in the sense that "if you just do these three things, then all will go well for you." No, not at all. However, it is a "how" book in the sense that, without a clear understanding of how to lead a true change process, we will just keep bouncing from one trend to the next, caught in an ongoing cycle of frustration, not understanding why our strategies are not working. What we've done in the pages to follow is simply a capturing or lassoing of the best practices of those who *have* led a successful change process.

This is our attempt to elevate a new conversation within children's ministry . . . to move the conversation from "yes, we need to change" to "here's the change process that's working for us. What change process has worked for you?"

You can count on part 1 (chapters 1, 2, and 3) to help you discern if you are *helping others see what you see.* That's where it starts. In these chapters we will break down how to attain ministry clarity so that others will understand what you aim to accomplish. Part 2 (chapters 4, 5, and 6) helps you *influence the grander vision of your church* as you engage ministry leaders throughout your church. We will examine how being a student of your senior pastor and building strong partnerships in your church will increase your alignment to the grander vision of the church—and ultimately improve your ability to implement ministry plans that are embedded in the core of your church mission. Part 3 (chapters 7, 8, and 9) will help you examine your unique leadership voice and learn how "leading from within" is central to your work serving God as a change agent in kidmin leadership. And, as mentioned, we've included a discussion guide at the back of the book that you can dig into by yourself or with your team.

If you only glean *one thing* from this book, know that true, influential, and transformational leadership takes place because somewhere a gritty leader decides, "With God's help, I'm gonna figure this out. I'm not gonna give up. I'm going to stay humble and figure out how to partner with and serve those below me, beside me, and above me to fulfill and extend the mission of this church." That's you. The Holy Spirit has the power to shape you and me to become that type of a leader.

THE ANGST AND ADVENTURE OF CHANGE

Change disrupts—and we all respond differently. Some of us run toward change like it's a doughnut shop on Saturday morning. Some of us hide under our desks when we hear its footsteps coming. Still others of us embrace change when it's convenient but resist it when it makes us feel uncomfortable. Truth be told, we probably are a little of all three in different seasons in our life!

There was a time, in the Garden, when we were so aligned with God that there was no need for transformative change. Adam and Eve walked in peace with God, and every need imaginable was met in Him and by Him. But the moment we chose our own path apart from God, sin and death became humankind's common enemy. We needed a rescue, an escape, a solution. We needed a change. Thankfully, the gospel was announced in advance, as recorded throughout the Old Testament, and fulfilled in the person and life of Jesus Christ . . . and this need for change was and is met in Christ. *Thanks be to God for this indescribable gift!*

Change is at the center of the Christian experience. Let's think about this together for a moment:

- Christ identified Himself as the *new* covenant in Luke 22.
- Paul tells us in Romans 12 to be *transformed* by the renewing of our minds.
- Jesus tells us in John 15 that He cuts off our branches that do not bear fruit. He also prunes the branches that do bear fruit so we can keep growing. Ouch! Double whammy in the name of change!
- Jesus said to *repent* in Matthew 4.
- Second Corinthians 5 tells us that anyone who is in Christ is a *new* creature . . . this is good news!

The very premise of the gospel is that we have a problem that only Christ can solve. And for those who are in Christ, we have been forever transformed, *changed* by the power of the gospel. The life of the Christ follower is one of worshiping God and proclaiming the *change* that Jesus has provided in our life and destiny as we engage with the community around us.

THE NEED FOR A CHANGE AGENT
(AHEM, THAT'S YOU)

The need for you to be a change agent is greater than ever. God hasn't changed. The gospel hasn't changed. Humankind's need for the gospel hasn't changed (we have needed it since Genesis 3:15). The Bible hasn't changed. But our culture has and is changing dramatically—and the way we engage with kids and families in our church is changing more rapidly than ever before.

There used to be a day when what was happening at the church was the biggest opportunity in town, or at least it was in the running for the time and attention of those in your church community. The amount of influence the church once had in the lives of its families was far greater in previous decades. We weren't as busy. We weren't as saturated in media. Fewer voices competed for our attention. Now, our robust economy, sports, music, and educational systems in Western society give kids, students, and families more opportunity than we could ever possibly take advantage of.

My (Matt's) family recently moved to Chicago's far western suburbs, where my sons have access to every type of musical opportunity imaginable (individual, performance, band, etc.), every type of sports league (if they show it on ESPN, we have it in a variety of competitive environments), robotics club, technology club, a variety of agricultural clubs, a variety of social/political clubs, community service clubs, career interest clubs . . . whew! I'm exhausted just listing those out!

But this isn't just my community; this is our community, our society, our culture, and our online world, where nearly any conceivable opportunity is a click away. These pressures, these voices, these involvements are shaping the thoughts and behaviors of parents, oftentimes far more powerfully than the church's call to be a disciple of Christ.

To complicate matters further, those of us in the church who are "on the ground" with families, children, and students often sense the need to change the way we engage with families far sooner than those who do not work as closely with them. These leaders don't see what we see. So what do we do? How do we process this frustration? How do we communicate this need for change to our senior pastor? How can we work with other key leaders in the church to solve these complex and systemic challenges to be good stewards and leaders of the gospel ministry? Try another "solution in a box"?

Or is the solution less about a program, and more about us?

You're probably reading this book right now because you have some level of frustration . . . or maybe because you lead a team and you want to raise them up as leaders. You've figured out that the challenges you're wrestling with require solutions that fit you, your team, your needs, your kids—not the plug-and-play, one-size-fits-all ideas you picked up at a conference or on a kidmin blog. Real solutions to real problems are harder—but more life-giving. Sometimes, the best word you can hear is the most painful word. And sometimes the most painful words are the most loving words (Proverbs 27:6a).

It's with this spirit that we'd like to gently whisper to your heart right now and say this: The solution you are looking for is not in a program or a curriculum; it's in a new posture of kidmin leadership. And with this new posture of leadership, you can walk the pathway ahead. Come, explore it with us in the upcoming pages.

God isn't calling trends to be the game changer—He's calling you.

PLUS . . .

IN ADDITION to our own years of experience, we have chosen to validate and support what we have learned by conducting quantitative research in which 340 kidmin leaders participated to give us a solid information and data source to pull from.

To help influence effective leadership, we are also giving you a tool called the Kidmin Dashboard (which will be introduced later in the book) that will help you implement what you are learning, as you learn it. Oftentimes we read a book, then have to go and figure out how to translate the strategy from that book into tools that will drive the strategy and tactics forward in our own unique context. With Leading KidMin *we are giving you a free, downloadable tool to help you lead change from your kidmin seat while you discover proven strategies to increase your effectiveness. Let's keep moving!*

Part 1

HELPING OTHERS SEE WHAT YOU SEE

Leading change in the local church is usually a process bathed in prayer—not a one-time event. We've learned from our decades of children's ministry experience, as well as by observing kidmin and local church colleagues from around the world, that the first step in making change happen is to help others see what you see—to gain clarity about your vision and to be able to share it with others.

Part of what it means to be a kidmin leader is to *influence* those who work on all sides of you; sometimes that even means your senior leaders. But what does it take to earn the respect of others so they will listen to you? What if your church hires a new senior leader—what will it take for you to earn favor with your new senior pastor?

This is the difference between leading with influence versus leading with power. While you may have the positional power to make things happen, the most effective leadership comes through influence. And influence is earned.

As you read through the next three chapters, consider what type of posture it will take to get your ministry right, to the point where you can drive, influence, and implement change on a larger scale, for God and His glory. Ask God to help you be open, honest, and willing to get gritty. That's what it will take to have the right to influence the grander vision of your local church. God's got this, and He's got you.

1

Break Out of the Vicious Trend Cycle—and Lead!

All I could see was the number of parents leaving their children's spiritual training completely up to us, the local church.

What was God trying to tell me?

Receiving a phone call from a parent can stir up so many different emotions. But this phone call was different. The parent wasn't calling to "recommend" a change for his child within our ministry. He wasn't calling with complaints or questions about a volunteer. He was calling because he was confused and filled with sadness over his nineteen-year-old, college-freshman son. Why call the kidmin leader? Because he knew that his child had had a significant turning point toward Christ in his faith journey when he was nine years old. But now, instead of living a life of putting God's Word into practice, standing unshakeable when the floods and torrents of life struck, his son was making choices that were pushing him toward destruction.

Ring. Sigh. Sadness. Discouragement. How long would this pattern continue?

I (Pat) would like to say that was the only parent phone call I received of its kind, but that would be far from the truth. Instead of dreaming of new horizons our children's ministry could explore, I found myself wrestling with God over the stories being told. This wrestling brought many sleepless nights. I found myself in the same state as these parents—confused and filled with grief and sadness over the kids who had made decisions for Christ in our children's ministry now walking away from their faith as they became older. During this time, I was asking a lot of questions. What did this mean? How could I help our church be more effective at making disciples? Was there anything I could really do to change things in our church? Was I alone?

Kids ministry leaders are gripped profoundly to make sure kids develop to be unshakeable in their faith. We want to make sure their life will never veer off course. We believe those wide-eyed, giggly preschoolers are full of potential! We believe every kid we lock eyes with matters to God, and they matter to us. Children's ministry leaders like you do the gritty, hard work of maximizing the resources we have been given to make our ministry the best children's ministry possible. We work hard to develop volunteers as fully functional leaders. We teach the Bible creatively with passion and clarity. Why? Because our desire is to inspire kids toward a transformed relationship with Jesus!

Your kids ministry and mine have shifted from "babysitting" kids to influencing and leading them toward spiritual growth. We find validation in and cheer the Barna Group as they share a statistic from their research that 80 percent of those accepting Jesus as their Savior do so before they turn thirteen. We take every opportunity we have to cast a vision to our volunteers of the importance of building relationships with our kids in a small-group environment so that they can learn how to apply God's truth to their everyday lives.

Much like you, my cheering turned into groaning when I heard through conferences and researchers like Orange, D6, Lifeway Research, and Christian Smith that a high percentage of college-age students who grew up in a church are walking away from their faith, having decided the church and their faith are not for them at all. It was at one of these conferences that I also heard George Barna share another staggering statistic from a national tracking survey entitled TweenPoll. This survey revealed that "only one-third of America's adolescents ardently contend that Jesus Christ returned to physical life after His crucifixion and death on the cross. By their own admission, they are confused theologically and do not know what to think about competing worldviews and belief systems." How could this be the outcome with the work we are doing? What part do you and I have in these statistics becoming the reality of our kids?

Bitterness was starting to creep into my groaning, which only gave Satan what he wanted. To crush these statistics, I decided to cast a new vision to our volunteers.

CRUSH THE STATISTICS!

I remember the gasps that came out the mouths of our volunteers as I asked ten kids, known to all of us, to walk on the stage, and then had eight of the ten kids actually turn their backs to the volunteers. This stark visual showed us that even with all the great work we were doing, some of these statistics could be a reality at our church. One volunteer yelled out, "Not on my watch it won't!" which brought the loudest cheer I ever heard from the rest of the volunteers! Some immediately began to get on their knees and pray. It didn't take long before everyone joined in lamenting before God to protect our kids and open our eyes. There wasn't a dry eye in the house! I remember opening my eyes as I listened to their prayers. I was moved to tears in thanking God for being a personal God, One who hears every prayer. I left that volunteer gathering knowing God had more for us to learn and face as a ministry.

I found myself searching Scripture to find courage and God's direction. It was during one of my Bible readings that I sensed God was speaking to me—and now it was time to see if I had the guts to obey. There were three words at the beginning of Deuteronomy 6:4 that

God wouldn't let me move from: "Hear, O Israel." I remember thinking, "Really God, You don't think I can handle more than these three simple words?" But the work that God had to do within me began with just those three words.

Have you ever found yourself only seeing a certain type of car on the road when you find yourself shopping for that particular car? Children's ministry became like this for me; I kept noticing the same thing over and over, every which way I turned. Even though our ministry was doing a dynamite job of helping kids know who God is by knowing His story, and volunteers were engaging kids through relationships, all I could see was the number of parents leaving their children's spiritual training completely up to us, the local church.

I remember the morning I cried with the realization that I, Willow's kidmin leader, put us (the church) in the posture of *owning* the responsibility of impressing God's commands on the hearts of the kids walking through our ministry doors. I remember sitting with my journal and I felt God lovingly tell me again, "Hear, O Israel." This is what I wrote in my journal next. *"I love your kids more than all your volunteers combined. Just as I spoke and moved the larger community of Israel, you must do the same. At times this journey will be difficult, requiring your perseverance, but know I have already put a community around you. It's your time to learn how to influence them."*

I believe many of us find ourselves clinging to the trend-solutions shared at all the big kidmin conferences, hoping that we will find some solution to our massive problem. Why? Because we know for the sake of our kids' spiritual development, something *needs* to change. Matt and I agree! We can "imagine the impact when church and family collide," as Reggie Joiner of Orange puts it.

> **All I could see was the number of parents leaving their children's spiritual training completely up to us, the local church.**

WE'RE DOING EVERYTHING RIGHT, BUT . . .

I (Pat) wanted to change the landscape of our ministry so that the stories of kids walking away from their faith after they left their homes and entered adult life were at a minimum, not a maximum. So, I did what many of us in the kidmin community do—I believed if I just implemented one of these out-of-the-box solutions to the walking-away problem, our ministry would be magically transformed. We would have parents begging us to be involved with what their children were learning and experiencing. I remember walking out of a macro-trend conference thinking that a particular solution presented was the game changer I had been searching for!

Here's the deal, I had an immediate need; the conference was *the* event that opened my eyes to see a significant shift was needed. So what did I do? I rallied my team together to wordsmith. We redrafted our mission statement, values, and purpose to align with this shift. Then we deployed them into action. Sound familiar?

Weeks turned into months, but the stories remained the same. How could this be? Our kid ministry added the programs I learned in the conferences showing a new way of ministry, a new trend-solution. Our strategies had all the right language but not much changed. What gives?

The problem was I believed *it* (the trend-solution) was the game changer. But God was looking to *me* to be the game changer. God was asking me to lead kidmin differently. *Hear, O Israel . . .* But how was I going to break away from this vicious cycle of getting caught up in out-of-the-box trend-solutions?

Effective kidmin leaders do the difficult work of understanding the deeper conversations behind the trend before rushing to implement the suggested trend-solution into the local church. Unfortunately, far too many kidmin leaders (myself included!) have been tempted to embrace the latest trend and neglect larger and deeper discussions.

Without seriously considering the impact on our ministry and receptivity of leadership to implementing the next given trend-solution, we are essentially setting the playlist on repeat . . . we will be here again soon.

We can break out of this seemingly endless cycle. But it will take a vulnerable level of honesty and listening, a deeper level of dialogue, and a different posture of leadership to change the game.

WHAT HAPPENED TO MY STATION WAGON?

We can learn a lot about the positive and negative impacts of trends just by watching what's happening in the marketplace. I (Matt) have vivid memories of growing up in the early 1980s and riding in the back of my parents' grand station wagon . . . facing backwards. Oh yeah, if your parents had one of these too, you know just how awesome this really was. It was like a whole different universe way back there in the rear-facing third seat. And since my brothers didn't want to ride facing backward, I was master of my own little universe.

Now if you were born in the mid-'80s or after you may not realize the immensity of these bad boys. These cars were *HUGE*. These vehicles were so massive they gave them extra-long names like *"Chevrolet Caprice Classic Station Wagon"* or *"Ford Country Squire XL Station Wagon."* Seriously? Someone in the marketing department fell asleep. Why not *"Behemoth"* or *"The Ultimate Grocery Getter"*? I guess they left the nicknaming up to third graders like you and me.

It was a very sad day when I got off the school bus, sometime around 1984, and ole Grocery Getter was gone. Nada. Zip. No longer in the driveway. Chrysler had done a very, very bad thing. What was this new maroon vehicle with the faux-wooden panels running down the side? Was it a full-size van that had been zapped by a shrink ray? Was it a K-Car with an abnormally tall roof and a hatchback? Nope, it was the beginning of a new revolution in the auto industry called the *minivan*.

A new macro-trend was born.

Enter: minivan, stage right.

Exit: station wagon with large rear-facing seat, stage left.

Crushed: my transportation fantasy world.

It's not difficult to think back over the past few years and consider how other marketplace (and local church!) trends have shaped the way we live our lives in the Western world. We now watch movies on small, handheld, portable devices, @tweeting our #FavoriteLine from the #Movie while locating on Urbanspoon where we are going to meet for dinner, Periscoping our dessert for seventy-three creepy, mostly unknown viewers, tracking our steps home on our Fitbit, then posting our final step-count on Instagram.

That sentence would not have made sense seven years ago, but somehow that all makes sense to us now. We are all "early adopters" now. But if we are not careful as kidmin leaders, we can adopt new trend-solutions before we have had the opportunity to talk candidly about what will be most effective for our local church context.

BUILDING A GRANDER VISION

Because of these challenges we all face in children's ministry, we are so desperate for a solution that we tend to fall back into a "coordinator" mindset, and we move too quickly into solution mode and invest too little time understanding and driving real, transformational, or systemic change. But actually solving the plethora of challenges we face takes a whole lot of creative grit. Because, as we've seen, what our churches really need are leaders willing to pay the price to help bring about authentic and systemic change.

God began to show me (Pat) that I needed to be a bit scrappy and do the hard work of taking great thoughts and strategies (like the suggested trend-solutions of family ministry, equipping parents, faith at home, and many others) and become the game changer or change agent needed in my local church! (We will unpack what this process looks like chapter by chapter as we continue through the book.) God was challenging me to let go of being the coordinator of "what is" (programs and out-of-the-box solutions) to becoming the leader and influencer who can align to a *grander vision* for our church to maximize our churchwide impact. His desire was for me to influence other ministry partners and open the eyes of church leadership if we were going to get radically different results.

Is God telling you the same?

THE IMPORTANCE OF DEFINING SUCCESS

This revelation helped me selectively abandon what wasn't working. Let me give you an example. After leaving a trend-solution conference, we came home and began creating *"FX": A Family Experience.* *"FX"* was a monthly gathering that immediately followed our weekend services in which kids sat with their parents to creatively learn biblical truths through worship, drama, and games. This event was well attended and totally fun! From the outside looking in, you would have thought that *"FX"* was a huge success!

Sounds like we should keep this, right? Surprisingly, no. The vision was great and families continued to attend, but it was a strategy owned *only* by our children's ministry, not our church leadership. Therefore, it didn't totally align with the overall strategy of our weekend church calendar.

Personally, I loved creating *"FX"*! I didn't want to stop *"FX,"* but I knew if I didn't manage my fear and courageously end its existence, I would continue being a coordinator of my strategy to address the trend instead of being God's game changer to bring about real change on a larger scale. Here's what I learned: *Before you implement a trend-solution, know what it is that will make that solution a winning strategy.*

Where I went wrong was, I didn't spend enough time defining what success was in my local church context before we went right into implementation mode. My first step should have been to pull the volunteers that I would consider core to our ministry and ask them how we would know if the trend-solution we wanted to implement was successful for us. If I had conducted deeper dialogue, not just with my kidmin team, but with other key partners within our church (our junior high pastor, high school pastor, and so on), discussing questions like "What do I really want out of this?" and "What will be key indicators of success?", it would have helped me identify possible gaps up front. It also would have engaged other strategic partners in the church to join this trend-solution into making it a reality that lasts.

It was very difficult to let "*FX*" die. But it was a necessary ending if we were going to head true north toward *our entire church* owning the vision of doing whatever it takes to crush the statistics and transform the hearts of our parents and kids to become champions of faith.

THINK ABOUT IT

WHEN IT COMES TO problem solving in leadership, where do you see yourself? Are you more of a coordinator who regularly finds yourself in a reactive mode based on the needs of the church calendar? Do you find yourself looking for the perfect game-changer trend or the out-of-the-box solutions? Or are you coming to realize that you must develop the skills to become the game changer to influence and drive more strategic and systemic change? No matter which group you most closely identify with, you are a part of the kidmin leadership struggle!

Most of us are in kids ministry because we are focused on the long-term vision of what we are trying to accomplish in the lives of children twenty years from now. What will their little lives look like when they are in college, as they start a family, as they make big life decisions? Will living for our great God be the central organizing principle of their lives?

What's unique about this book is, it is a resource you can use every year to rethink the way you do ministry so you accomplish your long-term vision. This book can become your personal tool for change, or it can be a tool used with your team to spur on conversations to help you manage the present and create a future together.

You *can* break the vicious cycle of running from one trend-solution to the next. In this chapter, we started by confessing that we've all done it. In the introduction, we declared that these trend-solutions alone would not solve our problem; rather, we need a new posture of kidmin leadership. In the chapters ahead we will walk through a more systematic way of leading within kidmin that will address the problems we face on a deeper, more authentic level—leadership that can bring about the church-wide impact you are looking for. It's hard work. It takes grit, determination, humility, and honesty. Let's do this together.

2

Gaining Clarity: For Yourself, For Others

The most important thing to remember is that in our line of work—in church settings in general—we're not in this alone.

Courtney walked out of the Executive Team meeting with fellow ministers feeling discouraged, confused, and wounded. How could that meeting have gone so badly? After all the work she had accomplished making sure the children's ministry had a clearly defined purpose, mission, vision, and values . . . yet she felt so misunderstood. So misrepresented. How could the children's ministry be so misunderstood after all of the work she had put into mission clarity? What had she done to lose favor with her senior leaders? Oh, the pain. She didn't know if she wanted to stew, cry, or walk away. Was it worth it?

Courtney (I've changed her name) is a friend of mine from California. She's a sharp kidmin leader. She's got a great education. She has fifteen years in local church kidmin experience. She's spoken in workshops. Her peers look upon her as a leader. Her heart for Christ, kids, and families is second to none. She works hard to make sure she has her stuff in order—my friend is organized! But there was something deeper about being a kidmin leader that God was trying to tell Courtney. And it's the same thing that He had told me (Pat) a few years earlier in my journey.

During this season of Courtney's ministry, this painful event was just one catalytic moment in a string of occurrences that helped Courtney see that ministry clarity isn't only about having your mission, vision, and values in order. No, it's much more than that. Don't get me wrong! You *must* have your mission, vision, and values in order, well documented, and embedded into the culture of your ministry. But the new way of leading Matt and I are talking about goes much deeper—and so many leaders miss it. Let's unpack it together.

WHAT COURTNEY WAS MISSING . . . AND WE MIGHT BE MISSING IT, TOO

When Courtney was brought on as the children's ministry leader, the church was running just under 400 in weekend attendance. Now, fifteen years later, the church was running around 1,500 on a weekend. Over this time period some of the founding staff members had moved on to other roles outside of their local church, her own responsibilities have grown, and she now has a couple of staff members of her own (one full-time assistant and a couple of part-time). With growth, change happens, right? I remember being on the phone with Courtney one April morning when she said, "You know, it's almost like the crazy-hectic pace of what I'm doing now is so chaotic that I've lost all perspective on what's going on, including my own leadership. I wonder if this has caused me to lose favor in the eyes of my lead pastor?" Click. Boom. That was it. "Let's keep digging under this one," I thought.

I remember being there myself as a kidmin leader . . . thinking I had everything right. Every "i" crossed and every "t" dotted (wait a minute, I may have gotten that backward), only to find out that there was more to being a church leader than I realized. Courtney had missed it, and for that matter, so had I earlier in my ministry. What was it that Courtney and I were not getting right? Two things. Let me shout them out for us really quickly. 1) Gaining perspective.

2) Finding favor. (Psst! Reread Courtney's statement, up above in the paragraph before this one . . . she pretty much nailed it. Ever been there? Are you there now? If you are not intentional, could you see yourself getting to this place?)

How does this work?

It starts with *ministry clarity*.

MINISTRY CLARITY: THE BASELINE

Ministry often starts with a dream or a vision for the future. But is your dream fuzzy to others, or is it crystal clear?

God often speaks to His people by helping them see a different future that will bring more glory to Him and will strengthen and extend the mission of the church. In February 2007, in a cabin outside of Gatlinburg, Tennessee, God gave me (Matt) the dream to launch the D6 Conference. For Pat it was in 2008, when God gave her the dream to create and launch a daycare center on her church campus for the church staff's kids.

With clarity about your kidmin dream, you will be able to determine your ministry's course and have the perseverance to impact and influence church leadership. Without clarity, you will find yourself being reactive, easily influenced. The energy and vitality that comes from pursuing God's dream for your ministry won't be there. You will focus on wanting to "win." When your dream does become a reality (and it will), recognize God has formed you through it and will also form others toward Him.

There is much more to be said about this, and our discussion guide in the back of the book includes questions that will help you take your dream to a greater place of clarity—so that others will understand you and help you bring about the results you are looking for. The most important thing to remember is that in our children's ministry line of work—in church settings in general—we're not in this alone. We can have the most amazing kidmin dream, but if we can't communicate it to others, it will stay a dream and never become reality.

Our first challenge is perspective.

GAINING PERSPECTIVE:
I WAS SO CLOSE I DIDN'T SEE IT

Have you ever gotten so close to an idea, situation, or even your work that you cannot see it clearly? I (Pat) used to have a boss who would say, "You are too close to your work and you are not seeing it clearly. You need to engage others into a deeper level of collaboration."

A few years ago I was driving on a local expressway, determined to get to my son's home so I could play with our grandkids before they headed to bed for the night. Even though I was traveling at the same speed as the cars around me, a driver behind me kept getting closer and closer. Have you ever been there? Now, the best defensive move I could have made was to move over and not become the source of the problem. I wish I could tell you that was exactly what I did to defuse the problem; but instead I found myself thinking what I was doing was right and this person was in the wrong. The way I saw the situation wasn't the way my tailgater saw it. Who was going to win?

We can have the most amazing kidmin dream, but if we can't communicate it to others, it will stay a dream and never become reality.

I realized my stress was rising! I have been told I can be strong-willed when I am focused on what I think is right, which can really frustrate those around me. Getting to my son's house safely but a little later than planned was more important than beating this "crazy person," so I finally decided to move over and let him pass me by.

Interestingly, he was focused on the road ahead, so he never tried to wave his "thank you" to me. How rude! Then I noticed we both exited at the same street. A few feet ahead, he quickly swerved into a driveway where I saw an ambulance parked with its lights flashing. Oh boy, I felt terrible!

From my seat, I saw a situation one way, and the person in the car behind me saw it another. Instead of defusing the situation, I had an urge to be the hero, making sure the story I was telling myself was validated. My emotions took over and became the villain in my own story.

That happened in a matter of minutes! Why? Because I got so close to a situation that I couldn't see it clearly. Because I wanted to be seen, understood, and validated for what I felt was important. Because I was too interested in what I felt was right instead of being open to another way of reaching the destination.

Truth be told, I have found myself with the same strong-willed mindset and triggered emotions when I felt church leadership didn't "get" the importance of kids ministry. *Why don't you see this?* What I have learned is there are different perspectives. When we all seek to understand and lead with unity to one common purpose, everyone can win!

GAINING PERSPECTIVE: GROWING YOUR SELF-AWARENESS AS A LEADER

I (Matt) have been blessed to work for three amazing ministries: Thomas Nelson Publishers, Randall House Publishers (the parent ministry of the D6 Conference), and Awana, a global children and youth ministry. After working for Randall House for eight years, I transitioned to Awana. Joining the Awana team was a wonderful experience and a relatively smooth transition, but I quickly learned that I needed to gain a new perspective on my leadership. When I came into Awana I assumed (subconsciously and unintentionally) that those around me knew my strengths and weaknesses. I assumed that I would be given the benefit of the doubt in certain situations. Guess what? This wasn't always the case! And you know what, that's my fault—not those around me. I lost perspective on how others were viewing 1) me as a leader, and 2) the ministry I was responsible for leading.

As kidmin leaders, if we want to drive significant change in the local church, we must be able to gain an honest perspective on our ministries and ourselves. This will take grit. It will require a different posture of leadership. But we can do this, with the help of the Holy Spirit and solid mentorship (more on mentorship in chapters 3 and 6).

Do you know your strengths, weaknesses, drives, personality, habits, and values as a follower of God and a kidmin leader? Your self-awareness is an essential first step toward maximizing your relationship with church leadership.

When Pat was driving the car from her own perspective, she wasn't very self-aware until she saw the flashing lights of the ambulance. It was then that she realized she was trying to control the situation. As she has shared this story with me, I remember her saying, "I wish that was the only time I fell short, but over the twenty-eight years of leading kids ministry, I had many times lost favor with church leadership because of being defensive, passive-aggressive, making excuses, and overcompensating for the work I was doing to try to show those in senior leadership and around me that I had my act together. I am in awe at how God chipped away at my insecurities, pointing me back to His love through Scripture."

For if anyone thinks he is something, when he is nothing, he deceives himself. Galatians 6:3

Who has spoken and it came to pass, unless the Lord has command-ed it? Is it not from the mouth of the Most High that good and bad come? Why should a living man complain, a man, about the punish-ment of his sins? Let us test and examine our ways, and return to the Lord! Lamentations 3:37–40

Every way of a man is right in his own eyes, but the Lord weighs the heart. Proverbs 21:2 (all ESV)

THINK ABOUT IT

SELF-AWARENESS is key to being an effective leader who knows how to engage effectively with others and how to influence the way other leaders think and act. Pat and I highly recommend the following tools as an investment in helping you become most aware of your strengths and opportunities as you engage with other leaders:

1. *StrengthsFinder*
2. *Myers-Briggs Type Inventory*
3. *Enneagram*
4. *A spiritual gifts assessment (various)*

You may have already taken one or more of these on your church leadership team, or you can find more information online or from a Christian counselor.

GAINING PERSPECTIVE: TOO BUSY TO THINK?

A few years ago when my (Matt's) boys were younger, we used to watch an Animal Planet show called *Meerkat Manor*. It was such a cute show, filled with adventure, learning, conflict, and even an occasional tragedy. While watching this show I noticed one thing about meerkats—they are always popping their heads up and down. It's both striking and adorable. Their life is like a constant dance of getting their faces down in the earth finding food, to popping up and looking out onto the horizon for threats and opportunities. They do this as a community, and when a threat is moving in on them, they are all poised and ready in an upright posture.

When I meet with kidmin leaders, I find that we spend so much time on the week-to-week, urgent items—getting ready for midweek or weekend kids ministry—we have no time to pop up and look out on the horizon for threats and opportunities. The pace at which we have to move to keep the plates spinning is concerning and at times even borderline unhealthy (you know who you are!).

I once heard a kidmin leader say, "Next Sunday is always staring me in the face." The pressure we feel to get the next weekend up and running with the right content/message, volunteers, and creativity can definitely keep us awake at night! This pace can keep us from seeing our ministry's strengths and weaknesses clearly. It can also bring the best leaders to a place of "copying creation." The first time I read this term was in a *Forbes* magazine article written by author Mike Myatt. He states, "The goal is to create, improve on, and innovate around *best* practices in order to find *next* practices."[1]

There have been times at Willow when I (Pat) found myself being a great copy creator! I would take great ideas from conferences and try to plug and play them in our ministry. My motive was pure because I believed in these best practices, but I wasn't seeing the start of any real big wins. So, how can I get out of this mode? What has to happen for me to pop up like our adorable meerkat friends and find the time and space to look at our threats and opportunities? In short, you need to clear your plates of those items that, when you don't do them, will have the least negative impact on your ministry.

Recently at Awana, I (Matt) found one of my teams in this exact predicament. Balls were being dropped. Deadlines were getting missed. The urgency of the week to week was eating us alive. This particular team's plates were so full, they didn't have the capacity to keep up with the demanding pace of the day to day, not to mention the ability to plan ahead, get ahead, have strategic conversations about the future, and have even deeper conversations around our culture, values, and leadership health. I sat down with the very capable director of this team and we decided the best decision was, for a season, to stop doing those things that, if

> **WE ALSO ASKED kidmin leaders: "For what purpose do you meet with your senior pastor?" To see the results to this question and for more access to the overall research project, go to Awana.org/LeadingKidmin/Research for the FREE download.**

they were stopped, would cause the least amount of collateral damage.

What? That's right. To do *more* of one thing is to do *less* of something else. Sometimes to get ahead (to pop up like a meerkat and look for opportunities or threats) you have to clear out the time and space to do so. And for us, this meant we needed to stop doing some tasks, for a season, so we could have some "strategic time" to devote to asking ourselves hard questions, doing more in-depth planning, and having future-oriented conversations about where we were headed as a team.

I think sometimes I wear my fast-paced ministry life as a badge of honor . . . only to realize that I'm limiting my long-term ability to drive strategic change forward. When sustained over long periods of time, this pace is unhealthy both physically and spiritually. There are a number of good books out there that explore these themes: *24/6* by Matthew Sleeth; *Margin* by Richard Swenson; *Sacred Rhythms* by Ruth Haley Barton. You might even want to read one of these with some of your team or others on your church staff.

Don't let your pace prevent the perspective you need to move forward. Choose to pop your head up like the meerkats and look for opportunities and threats. Clear your calendar of all that doesn't have to happen and find the time to think and process through the questions in the discussion guide in the back of this book.

A note of caution: If "clearing your calendar" temporarily means that the work of ministry teammates will be impacted, you will want to seek their approval before you just stop (or pause) doing something that will negatively affect them. You need to help them "feel your pain." Help them understand that if you don't create some space to address this, it will not be good for the long-term health of your ministry . . . and theirs. (You know, even your car needs an oil change every now and then. Oh boy, I was supposed to do that last week. Gotta run!)

FINDING FAVOR:
WHAT'S HOLDING YOU BACK?

Having the ability to see others' viewpoints, being open, being flexible, and acknowledging others might know more in certain areas to help accomplish our kids ministry mission will bring you favor from church leadership. Proverbs 3:4 reminds us true favor and high esteem are possible in the sight of God and man.

Does true favor mean we won't have challenges and opposition? Absolutely not! We all know challenges and opposition will come even when having the favor of God, but when opposition comes our way, are we taking time to reflect? Is your opposition coming because you are not seeing your ministry with the same perspective as your church leadership?

After facing some tough ministry moments with church leadership, I (Pat) decided it was time for me to ask for honest feedback of those around me. Oh boy! Brace yourself! I didn't find a feedback assessment tool online. I simply asked a third party to call some of my friends and a few family members to ask a few questions so that I could better understand how others perceived me. This was so incredibly tough! Tougher than tough. But it was worth the temporary pain to become a better leader. The questions and responses of friends and family were what brought me to my knees in asking God to help me change. Is it time for you to do a perspective reality checkup? If so, here are the questions we used.

1. How often does [insert your name here] have the ability to see other perspectives because she has a good understanding she is capable of making mistakes?
2. Share a time when [_____] apologized for her/his actions and did not blame others? Is this a natural response of hers/his?
3. Do you ever notice [_____] behavior changing due to stress? Does she/he notice it? Or does she/he defend her/his behavior as being right?
4. Do you find [_____] demeanor being defensive, controlling, passive-aggressive, and making excuses?

This is deep work. It's hard work. It's courageous work. Instead of taking their comments and burning them, I knew I needed to get at the real issues of "why I was the way I was" if I was ever going to become a change agent moving forward. Journaling, prayer, being vulnerable with my Christian counselor, and getting to the place of thanking my friends and family members for loving me to the point of being totally honest opened my eyes to my flaws. It brought me to a place of walking in freedom, knowing I am loved by the Most High God!

Not walking through this process may be the very thing that's keeping you from finding favor from leaders around you, and you may be blind to it. As a kidmin leader who wants to reach kids and equip families, if you truly want to take your ministry to the next level, this may be part of what's holding you back. Not a program. Not a strategy. You.

FINDING FAVOR:
"GETTING YOUR STUFF RIGHT"

I've been serving at Willow Creek Community Church for twenty-eight years. I'm at a place where I can say with humble confidence that I have found favor in the eyes of my senior pastor, Bill Hybels. But finding favor with my senior leader is something that took great discipline, grit, and a different posture of leadership from me as a kidmin leader.

THINK ABOUT IT

FOR A DEEPER look into the lives of these great biblical heroes on your own, consider reading about how God granted these men favor: Noah in Genesis 6, Joseph in Genesis 39, and Samuel in 1 Samuel 2.

These three men's credibility spread among those around them because of how they chose to respond in every situation. They had faith and absolute allegiance to God first, knowing God had perfect timing and a perfect plan even if the timing and outcome of His plan didn't align with their personal desires.

As I was researching for this book, I studied Noah, Joseph, and Samuel. Each found favor from God as he relentlessly pursued his mission. They inspire us to greater heights of leading. I was encouraged as I read how they lived their lives, followed God, and moved the mission He placed before them. Like them, we have favor with God. God's favor to you and me is constant. His favor gives us the grace and capacity to face any obstacle and have the courage to pursue clarity and purpose. What limits us from finding true favor from church leadership of our kids ministry mission?

Choosing the way we will respond in situations (like our fellow kidmin leader Courtney) will either attract or hinder the favor given to us from church leadership. So what exactly does it mean for us to "find favor" with our senior pastor or the senior leaders at our local church?

Granted, someone at your church, likely someone in leadership, hired you because they found some level of competency and trust in you. But let's not be mistaken—just because you were hired does not mean that you have already found favor with your leaders. Finding favor with a leader above you means gaining approval, acceptance, special benefits, or blessing. Finding favor is what Daniel-san received from Mr. Miyagi in *The Karate Kid*. It's what the King granted Mrs. Anna Leonowens in *The King and I*; and it's what Jane Eyre gained from Edward Rochester in the classic love story. Finding favor is gritty work. But how? Beyond prayer, healthy relationships, and hard work, what exactly has to happen for us to gain favor with our senior leaders?

I believe that finding true favor from senior leadership is possible for every kidmin leader when these two things are happening:

When the clarity of your kids ministry mission intersects with the vision of your church. This is making sure your children's ministry has extreme clarity around your purpose, mission, vision, and values. It's also making sure your children's ministry is aligned with the grander vision of the church. (More to come on this.)

When we have the courage to gain perspective and recognize our inner selves (our strengths and weaknesses). Kidmin leaders who have found favor with their senior leaders are men and women who have taken the time to understand how God created them, by a strong assessment of their gifts, assets, and strengths—as well as weaknesses, opportunities for growth, and potential blind spots. This takes grit! It takes a deep and vulnerable level of honesty and trust. This is part of that different posture of leadership we keep talking about.

Once you have found favor with senior leaders (and this can take a long time), then you've established a deeper level of trust and a warmer affection toward your voice and leadership. Finding favor is an indicator that you've "gotten your stuff right" . . . you have your ministry in order . . . you've earned the right to be heard. Not just because you did the right things but because you also invested the relational equity and you honed your own leadership.

Remember, finding favor is an indicator of something deeper you've been doing (with the Holy Spirit's help!) inside your own leadership world. Don't view favor as an external "to do" like completing a strategy or putting on an event. It's a slow process that requires discipline, clarity, self-reflection, transparency, prayer—all wrapped up in a lot of relational investment with the Lord and the leaders on all sides of you.

ARE YOU CAUGHT UP IN THE CURRENT?

A few years back, I (Matt) was with my boys launching sticks and rocks into the Ohio River while on a weekend getaway as a family. As you likely know, the Ohio River is long, wide, and powerful. When you cast a stick out far enough and it gets caught up in the current, you can watch the stick move swiftly downstream until your eyes can no longer distinguish it from the endless ripples in the dark, murky water. This is the sort of secret, cool stuff fathers and sons do together when Mom is not around. (Shh. Don't tell.) But my youngest son lacked the arm strength to get the stick out far enough; it wasn't quite getting caught up in the pull of the river current, so his sticks kept swirling near the edge of the river and the little alcoves created by years of erosion and land contour.

So I gave him a little help. Together we were able to launch the stick out far enough where it got caught up in the main current. Without my help, he was able to make it *in* the river, but his stick wasn't really moving . . . it was in the river, but just swirling near the banks. He needed my partnership to cast his stick out far enough to watch it really move downstream.

Is your children's ministry getting caught up in the primary current of your church—where it's clearly understood by the right partners (pastor, parents, leaders, volunteers, etc.)? Is it a part of the movement to reach people with the gospel and equip them as disciples? Or is your children's ministry not clearly understood (by you, your pastor, your leaders, volunteers, and parents) and being pushed to the margins, swirling near the banks?

We think every kids' pastor or children's ministry director wants their kids ministry to be part of the primary current of the local church ministry, because you see the value in reaching and discipling kids, and equipping parents to be partners in disciple-making. As a kidmin leader you likely see this as central to the mission of the church, not peripheral.

In order to move closer to this place where the children's ministry can be seen as a more strategic part of your local church ministry, you need to find out how others see your ministry. We will look further at this in the next chapter.

WHAT DOES THE RESEARCH TELL US?

In our research we asked our 340 respondents: "Please tell how clear you believe the vision and purpose for your church's children's ministry is to the following. Please answer using a 5-point scale where 1 is "Not clear at all" and 5 is "Completely clear."

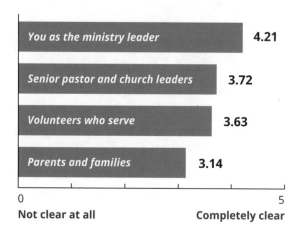

It always helps to see that the numbers support the story we know to be true anecdotally, because we face it week in and week out. As we can see from the research, the further away we get from the kidmin leader (the one responsible for the vision and purpose), the less clear the purpose of ministry can become. It may be that you have already understood this disparity to be true. And certainly Pat and I have understood this to be a common story among kidmin leaders and churches. So what do we do about it?

So much of our time in children's ministry is spent on reacting to church leadership decisions: church services and events come every week, and they come in rapid frequency! Kidmin leaders can find themselves managing the present, swirling near the banks, feeling like we can't join the primary energy and direction of the local church. So many leaders are unable to gain momentum from church leadership to create a future—a future that tells everyone within and outside of their church that kid ministry is not an afterthought but at the forefront of many, if not most, of the decisions impacting their church's future.

People in different positions see things differently. What you and

I see from our position is probably not seen the same way by church leadership. If we want to unlock the potential that exists in our kids ministry, we have to have extreme clarity with all of the right partners in our local church (like the pastor, other leaders, volunteers, and parents listed in the research results above). A key part in achieving this much-needed clarity is getting into the current of the grander vision of the church. We must be willing to see our ministry as those leading us see it in order to carry the vision farther downstream. But if we are going to do that, we need to take a look at what the research numbers in this section tell us and ask: what is it going to take to move those numbers upward?

What Pat and I are suggesting is that it's more than well-constructed mission, vision, and values statements that are built with the right strategic partners and alignment to the grander vision of the church. (Although this is extremely important, it is only the baseline.) The next step is being able to gain perspective to help you find favor with church leadership.

USING THE KIDMIN DASHBOARD

OKAY, LET'S BE HONEST, none of us really likes to go to the doctor. But when we are sick, we want to be able to "name it." And few of us like to stare at ourselves in the mirror, but when we need to look in the mirror we expect an honest reflection. The Kidmin Dashboard is a way for you and your team to get an accurate reading or reflection on how you are doing in some of these areas. We figured that you've been reading this chapter long enough, so we decided to make a video on the Kidmin Dashboard where we're going to walk you through how to use this extremely helpful and easy tool.

Want to track how well you are fulfilling your ministry purpose? How well you are finding favor in the eyes of senior leaders? How about how well your kidmin purpose is aligned with your church values? You can use this tool as a talking-point instrument and invite other leaders to help you track or rate where you are, determine what kind of progress you are making, and plan ahead three months at a time.

 To download the Kidmin Dashboard, and to watch a video of our shining faces, go to Awana.org/LeadingKidmin/Dashboard

3

How to Run Toward Your Problems

What obstacles might you be facing that hinder your ministry progress?

Nick noticed Scott, one of his best-prepared leaders, reacting with sarcasm toward a question one of the kids asked in his small group. Nick shrugged it off as Scott having a bad day. *Nick ran away from the problem.* Jessie, an infant volunteer, was walking into the infant room holding a cup of coffee. Sandy, the room leader, didn't say anything even though everyone knows there is a policy of not bringing hot beverages into any room with children. Sandy knew Jessie loved her morning coffee and there weren't many infants in the room yet. She hoped Jessie would be quick about finishing her drink. *Sandy ran away from the problem.*

John found himself getting frustrated with "big church" (you know—the adult service) because the service length kept increasing instead of staying consistent with the agreed-upon end time of the service. John watched the kids get squirrelly due to being tired and hungry. When John's supervisor asked him how the weekend went, John smiled and said, "It was great!" John *definitely ran away from the problem*!

Have you ever faced at least one of these situations as a kidmin leader? Have you ever found yourself making a choice to run away from "the problem" instead of running toward it and facing it directly?

"YOU HAVE A CHOICE TO MAKE"

I (Pat) remember the teenage years of our daughter. She was a great kid, but her teenage years were not what I would call "easy." For most parents, we find ourselves wanting to run away from home as we face multiple difficult conversations of curfews being broken, chores not getting done, and the "sassy rolling of the eyes" look. I remember thinking, "That's it! It is time to get our daughter some help because she's making our home life so difficult!"

I felt the best way to face this problem head-on was to bring her to a trusted counselor. I knew this counselor would tell her she was being unreasonable toward parents who loved her. The door finally opened as I sat in the waiting room. Our daughter walked out, hugged the counselor, and gave me a huge smile. Success!

The next morning the phone rang. It was the counselor on the other end, asking me if I had time to talk. I said, "Sure," with excitement, knowing she was going to tell me what a great job I was doing as a parent of a teenager! She began to explain how delightful our daughter is and how she has wonderful relational skills. She shared that my daughter's heart was filled with the gift of mercy that God instilled in her. I remember taking the phone away from my ear, wondering if the counselor had called the wrong number!

The next thing she said to me hit really hard. "Now, I am not saying your daughter is perfect. She is a typical teenager in need of boundaries. However, I don't feel she really has the problem in the relationship. You do. You have a choice to make. You can either run from the problem in your home or choose to face it head-on to learn the deeper reasoning behind it." Boom! Yowzas, that really hurt!

She then asked if I would be open to coming in for a conversation about me, not our daughter. I didn't want to run toward what she was going to share. All I wanted to do was run from hearing the truth . . . run far, far away.

Running from a problem and the truth comes in all shapes and sizes. Some of us run because life is moving so fast and we don't feel we have the time or energy to dive into what is really going on. Some run due to the heightened stress we feel. Some of us run because we think others are wrong and we are right. Others choose to run from a problem because if you run, you can deny the problem even exists. Many of us run because, even though we so deeply want to address the problem, we serve/work in an environment where honest, transparent critiques and feedback are not a part of the cultural fabric of our ministries. (It's endemic in ministry settings and Christian workplaces: we want to be "nice" to each other.) But you can be the change agent to help reshape your ministry culture by modeling the very thing that is so deeply needed.

I was talking with Carrie a few weeks ago about recent leadership lessons learned. She was sharing how difficult ministry was for her as she was trying to launch a new area of her ministry. It didn't take long for her emotions to well up in our conversation. Near the end of our conversation, she said, "I just didn't see how I was set up to win. I was trying to give my best, but when I don't feel trusted by leadership, I just want to run and quit."

My heart sank. Carrie is a wise leader. Shortly after we talked I had the opportunity to walk through her ministry spaces. As I watched, listened, and felt the excitement, I couldn't help but think what would have happened had Carrie run far away from the ministry because of the pain she felt in the process of leading.

Whatever makes us run from a problem, the journey to honesty and receptivity will be hard. My experience has shown me the journey can change your life and the outcome can be ranked as one of the best leadership experiences as you see God's grace and mighty hand at work!

JONAH, DAVID, AND US

Running toward the problem through hearing honest feedback was the best step I took in getting my ministry right. My personal and ministry experience has shown me running toward a problem will strengthen and challenge every leadership muscle within, bringing me to a place of true wisdom and a stronger, better me.

Running toward the problem brought me to a place of doing something I have never done before: finding the deeper meaning of why I chose to project my fears and insecurities onto our daughter. I gained insight showing me that I wanted to validate my running through *blaming the reason we were having problems on someone else.*

Jonah, a prophet in the Old Testament, blamed others for his problems as well. Instead of obeying God, Jonah and the ship's crew paid a costly price for Jonah making a choice to run away instead of running toward the problem facing the people of Nineveh. He was thrown into the sea, swallowed by a fish, and sat under a plant that was eaten by a worm, causing him to have discomfort from sitting in the blazing sun. Jonah's problems began when he chose not to follow the steps God laid before him. He ignored God, which created a much bigger problem. He felt justified in his reason to disobey God. We read about his pride, frustration, and envy. Why did Jonah think he was justified, or in the right, to run away?

Jonah grew up feeling a deep hatred for the people of Nineveh. His hatred was so strong, he would do anything to keep himself away from them. His desire for the people of Nineveh was for them to be destroyed by God. Jonah 4:1 tells us Jonah was very upset with them and with God. Why? He had a narrow view of God's mercy, wanting the wicked people of Nineveh to be destroyed. That's what they deserved—death and nothing more!

Jonah chose to forsake the mission given to him by God to face the people of Nineveh. Through every problem he faced, he ran thinking of himself and his own desires.

David, as a young boy, didn't run away from Goliath. He chose the courageous route and ran toward the problem facing him. David moved from being a giant-killer to king. As we read the Scriptures that explain his life as king, we read of the many problems he created because he was selfish, wanting to do life his way instead of God's way.

Take a look at 2 Samuel 12:1–25 in the Old Testament. David was given another opportunity to listen to someone. Nathan rebuked David by telling him a story reflecting David's own life. David, not realizing Nathan was talking about him in the story, found he "was furious. 'As surely as the Lord lives,' he vowed, 'any man who would do such a thing deserves to die! He must repay four lambs to the poor man for the one he stole and for having no pity'" (vv. 5–6). After Nathan explained he was actually talking about David by telling the story, David found himself in a place of realizing he had sinned against God. One of the many lessons we learn from studying David's journey of running from problems is *God greatly desires our complete trust and worship before, during, and after any problem we might face.*

RUNNING AS A TEAM

Many people say the journey of running is much easier when you run with others. I had the joy of running (well, actually walking) in a 5K race for hunger. The exercise wasn't the joy factor for me; it was the opportunity of participating side by side with adults with special needs. We made our final turn toward the end of the race, when one person got so tired he actually sat down on the ground and said he was done. The people behind just walked around us, continuing toward the finish line.

Every adult with special needs stopped and circled around our tired friend. With their words and gestures, they finally got him to stand. We were the last to finish the race, but we finished together!

When we read the book of Hebrews, we are reminded of those before us who finished together. We are not the first to struggle as we run in a race to face problems. Others before us have run the race and won.

Therefore, since we are surrounded by such a huge crowd of witnesses to the life of faith, let us strip off every weight that slows us down, especially the sin that so easily trips us up. And let us run with endurance the race that God has set before us. (Hebrews 12:1)

We are reminded we are not running as individuals, competing against one another. We are running as a team, helping the team to finish the race together, no matter what obstacles come before us.

What obstacles might you be facing that hinder your ministry or personal progress? What is or isn't keeping your endurance up to get to the finish line that God has set before you?

LISTENING: THE PAIN AND THE POWER

I want to take a turn in this section and share a hard ministry journey when all I could think to do was to run away and run fast! It all began when my team and I began working on our own Kidmin Dashboard.

One of my leadership team volunteers had a professional career as a strategic developer and consultant for mid- to large-sized corporations. He has always been known as a man who pressed with tough questions whenever asked. He would describe himself as someone who saw life half-empty instead of half-full. I, on the other hand, am definitely a half-full kind of gal! Even though I enjoy strategy and creating new ideas, our ministry needed Tim on our leadership team to balance my leadership.

Who do you have on your kidmin team that balances your leadership?

Well, the five of us gathered one Saturday afternoon. After sharing the vision of the Kidmin Dashboard, everyone attending was pumped to begin the conversation! I thought this was going to be a quick conversation and our three-month plan was probably going to be pretty simple to move forward. From my kidmin seat, I felt the problems we were having weren't our fault. We were clear; our problems would be fixed if leadership and our parents rallied with us! Boy, was I wrong!

Like getting stuck on the first agenda item of a meeting, we couldn't move past the first box of the dashboard: "Kidmin Purpose Reality." We all agreed the primary target audience that we were called to serve is kids, but we couldn't agree if we were truly reaching them in a way that brought them closer in their relationship with God. The lenses that influenced each person's perspective were based on personal stories.

Tim shared multiple stories of conversations he had with parents. Recently, he called the parents of two boys from his fifth-grade small group. Tim had noticed both boys' absence over the past three weeks and he wanted to check in. The parents of both boys had similar stories to share. Life was busy, and their families needed time to sleep in on Sunday morning. A dad finished the conversation by saying, "Hey, thanks for calling. We know the ministry will always be there, but for now, we just need to get through the craziness." Stories like these brought Tim to the conclusion that our mission needed to be more compelling to help parents make church a priority for their family.

Nancy said she disagreed. She felt we *were* offering compelling opportunities for children, but what she observed on the weekends gave her a different story. Nancy explained she continually observed the parents who pick up the kids in her room just want to get in and out. They aren't taking time at drop-off or pick-up times to talk with the volunteers who lead their kids. Nancy was brought to the conclusion we were clear, but family schedules take away our opportunity of truly reaching kids for Christ.

Ken, one of our large-group teacher-volunteers, felt the only way to satisfy these needs and disciple the kids we were trying to teach was to lengthen the time of the large-group program. His conclusion came from seeing the kids ask some tough questions about the content being taught. Ken felt if we extended the time we had with the kids, he would have more time to teach the kids. An extended time frame would tell parents what we were doing is important and kids would learn better.

Phil, our administratively minded volunteer, spoke from the stories he saw on the weekends. His role is to lead our safety teams and administrative teams. Phil and his team pay attention to volunteer recruitment, number of kids in small groups, our attendance numbers, and what he observes as families walk through our hallways. He said even though our weekend attendance was showing families are attending two times or less per month, our group leaders can't possibly minister to the hearts of the kids because their group size has grown 30 percent—because we don't have enough volunteers.

And Karen, a parent and small-group leader-volunteer, said, "I think parents are doing the best they can by dropping their kids off to us. Aren't we the kid faith-building experts in our church? Parents drop them off to the best soccer coaches to teach them skills. They drop them off to us so we can teach them about God and His Word."

Have you ever led a volunteer conversation that you felt was quickly getting away from you? Looking down at my watch, I realized we had been talking for three hours without much movement on our dashboard! It was time to stop the conversation and take a step back to validate if these were our ministry problems, or not.

So what did we do? As you can tell from this ministry story, listening can be messy. We had a choice to make. Were we going to work through the mess, hopefully coming out the other side with more strategic discussions and decisions, or were we going to throw up our hands and just put the blame of the mess on others?

We decided to work through the mess. We took out our calendars to pick a date three weeks later so that each of us could get quiet before God and ask Him for guidance. Three weeks later we were able to face the hard conversations again, with a peace in knowing God was about to lead us to deeper, more strategic discussions that would change everything.

WHAT'S THE PROBLEM?

Do you remember the story of my volunteer gathering shared in chapter 1, where we dramatized the problem of kids running from their faith? There *is* a lot at stake; however, instead of digging deep to see what our ministry was doing that limited the kids from being steadfast in their faith, it was easier for me to blame church leadership, our parents, and the culture for our ministry's shortcomings.

My mentor challenged me to do what was needed to seek the best knowledge and wisdom that I could. I remember thinking I needed to have the courage to stop and ask wise people to show us where we were strong as a ministry, but more importantly, where we were weak in accomplishing our mission. I would not have arrived at this level of openness to fix our systemic problems had I not been vulnerable enough to listen to those around me to begin with. Listening to my team helped me to see the signs that we had a problem that needed to be solved.

> **It was easier for me to blame church leadership, our parents, and the culture for our ministry's shortcomings.**

Successful kidmin leaders don't run away from ministry problems; they pursue knowledge. And processing knowledge can turn into true wisdom, but this only happens by first recognizing we must be willing to ask hard questions and listen to difficult responses. Proverbs 27:6a says, "Faithful are the wounds of a friend" (ESV). Those who truly love you and your ministry may say things that are difficult to hear, but it may be those very words of wisdom that lead you forward.

WHAT DOES THE RESEARCH TELL US?

SO HOW ARE WE DOING as a kidmin community in the area of feedback, asking questions, and listening? In our research in the area of feedback, we were somewhat encouraged, yet we have room for improvement, as you can see from the accompanying data. We asked leaders, "How open are you to others giving you feedback and evaluation on your children's ministry?" Respondents rated themselves on a 5-point scale, with 1 being "not open at all" and 5 being "very open."

On the encouraging side, 57.34% rated themselves as a 5 (very open to feedback). To think that over half of those in children's ministry leadership are very open to receiving feedback is encouraging! Plus, an additional 30.47% rated themselves a 4, which tells us the vast majority of our respondents are warm toward others giving feedback. Only 12.19% rated themselves a 3, 2, or 1, indicating that about 1 out of 10 inside of the kidmin community are less warm and more closed to receiving feedback from others.

HOW OFTEN ARE WE
ACTUALLY RECEIVING FEEDBACK?

But how often are we "actually receiving" feedback? By asking two distinct questions, we acquired a clearer picture of where we actually are. Check out the results.

Receiving Feedback Question 1. *How often have you*

invited outside experts (teachers, theology professors, other children's ministry leaders, other ministers, etc.) in to give you feedback and evaluation of your ministry?

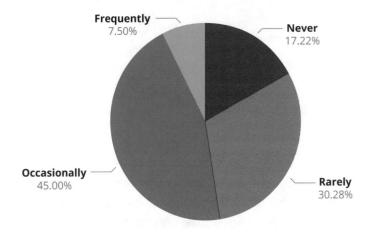

Frequently 7.50%

Never 17.22%

Occasionally 45.00%

Rarely 30.28%

BY FAR, THE MOST concerning finding here is that 47.5% (that's almost 5 out of 10) of kidmin leaders are not pursuing knowledge and critiques from outside of their own local churches. Although, oftentimes, our needs and solutions are somewhat contextualized to our own local church culture, there is a wealth of knowledge outside of our own church. By inviting trusted and proven leaders, we can gain greater wisdom and knowledge to increase our learning and growth to be better stewards of the ministries God has entrusted to us. Kudos to the 52.5% who are frequently or at least occasionally facing outward! How about you? Are you seeking outside feedback to help your ministry get stronger?

Receiving Feedback Question 2. *How often have you invited those you respect and value within your local church to give you feedback and evaluation of your ministry?*

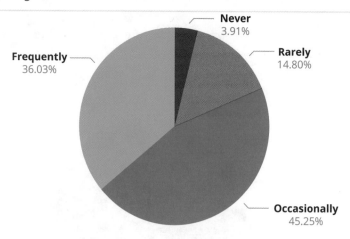

THE ENCOURAGING finding here is that, within our own local church contexts, we are not only comfortable, but we are somewhat active in engaging others within our church in gathering feedback. 81.28% are either frequently or occasionally receiving feedback from trusted individuals within our churches. On the flip side, almost 2 out of 10 (18.71%) are rarely or never receiving feedback from those within our own ministries.

Where do you fit within the spectrum? Are you pursuing and seeking feedback from trusted individuals inside and/or outside of your ministry? If so, how often? I always thought I was open to pursuing knowledge by listening to others, but continue reading.

CHOOSING THE BEST PEOPLE

Knowledge, the accumulation of facts and data, is what God used to show me I couldn't keep our ministry spinning with uncertainty. If I really wanted to engage church leadership buy-in, I needed to get it right within our kids ministry first. It was time to stop being defensive and *reach out to others* outside of our ministry who are much wiser than I.

If I chose people who had similar thinking to me to observe and give me ministry feedback, I would have been choosing wrong. The best people to give us the wisest ministry feedback are the people who can be objective, clear, and can challenge our thinking. I began my search for this new team by first going to God.

The writer of Psalm 42 was discouraged. *Why am I discouraged? Why is my heart so sad? I will put my hope in God!* Verse 5 reminded me to remember God's goodness and to have hope He will lead me to the best people whom He has already chosen for me. And God did just that!

I found myself in conversations asking people who they felt were the best spiritual formation experts of kids. I also asked others who were the best educational experts within our school districts. Once I had a list of names and prayed over them, I started reaching out to each person to ask them to come visit our ministry. If this feels like a daunting task for you, consider asking one of your key volunteers to help you make these connections. The important thing is to not give up! Remember, God will open the doors, and He has the perfect timing of when you will meet with whom He is bringing forward.

Within one month's time, I had two spiritual formation experts for kids and one educational expert who agreed to meet me for coffee. I knew if I could get them excited about the task at hand and to see my heart wanting to learn, they would agree to give of their time and wisdom. (If this sounds more complicated and time-consuming than would work for you, choosing even one outside "expert"—say, a local teacher you respect—would still be helpful.)

We agreed upon how many weekends each would observe and when I would sit with them to hear "the truth." Before they arrived to observe our ministry, I introduced them to my leadership team. They were given full access to our ministry.

Now, let me be clear. As I look back to the beginning of this journey, I was a prideful leader. Yes, I wanted their feedback because I knew we had a few problems, but I thought they were going to find minimal changes needing to be made. I still wanted to blame our problems on someone else. Little did I know God wanted me to face the problem head-on to learn the deeper reasoning behind it.

The time came to hear their thoughts. The spiritual formation experts began by asking me if I believed God spoke to kids today. Did I think He was real and intimately involved in their everyday lives? I thought that was an odd way to start our meeting, but I looked them straight in the eye and said, "Absolutely!"

Without hesitation, both said, "We wouldn't have thought that would have been your answer because you move kids quickly from activity to activity, not giving them time to stop and hear what God might be telling them." I remember thinking, "Have you ever worked in a children's ministry before? Do you know if you don't move them quickly behavior problems will arise? Moving them fast will limit the number of behavior problems we have to deal with!"

They continued to share what was holding us back from being a thriving ministry with a clear mission to help the kids coming our way to move closer in their relationship with Christ. I had a choice to make. Was I going to allow this to strengthen and challenge every leadership muscle within me, or was I going to run from it?

You already know I felt like running, but God greatly desires our trust. No one loves our children more than God! I had to find out why I was having difficulty in trusting Him and believing He was speaking through the experts. Was I finding my worth in our ministry and not in God? I remember feeling my validity as a leader was going to be tarnished if their comments were found to be true. Oh, how God showed me I was letting ministry become my identity.

At the same time I began this journey of discovering my insecurities, I asked Felix, a man in our congregation, to do a deep dive to find out our parents' perception of our ministry and how we were doing in partnering with them in laying a spiritual foundation for their kids. It was in these conversations with Felix the parents shared the external factors pulling on them to sporadically attend church. They were honest because Felix was in a position to listen. Having Felix lead parent focus groups was one of my better decisions. The parents shared their kids felt shamed by their volunteer leaders if they were not in church. As I dug into this further with our volunteers, we were able to name what was broken, apologize where needed, and create the best next steps to move forward.

The journey continued to be difficult as I heard ways to improve, but I have experienced answers to my prayers. When I took every comment, every frustration, and every cry to God, He heard and answered.

I love the Lord because he hears my voice and my prayer for mercy. Because he bends down to listen, I will pray as long as I have breath! Death wrapped its ropes around me [these comments felt like I was going through a ministry death]; *the terrors of the grave overtook me. I saw only trouble and sorrow. Then I called on the name of the Lord: "Please, Lord, save me!"* [Save our ministry. Save what is good, what is right, what is of You so that our kids move closer to You.] *How kind the Lord is! How good he is! So merciful, this God of ours!* (Psalm 116:1–5)

IT TAKES COURAGE, AND YOU'VE GOT WHAT IT TAKES!

Have you ever observed that when one leader has the courage to take a step forward, it makes it easier for the next leader to follow? I (Matt) think that Pat's courage to do the difficult thing will inspire others, possibly you, to be willing to *listen honestly, when you just want to run.*

Pat and I both live in the Chicago suburbs where Canada geese rule the skies (and the public parks . . . watch your step!). Canada geese fly in a V formation—the one in the front can carve out a path by pushing the air molecules aside so that each subsequent goose has less air resistance to cut through. Every so often the lead goose falls back and another takes her place in the front. In much the same way, Pat, and other kidmin leaders like Pat, have cut a path before you, showing you that you too can have the courage to zoom up to that front position to take on a little bit of wind resistance as you do the difficult thing of listening to difficult feedback. You can do this!

Let my soul be at rest again, for the Lord has been good to me. He has saved me from death, my eyes from tears, my feet from stumbling. And so I walk in the Lord's presence as I live here on earth! (Psalm 116:7–9).

And so can you! Have a full view of God's mercy. He will give you the courage to run toward any ministry problem you might have that is holding the ministry back from accomplishing its vision. Remember where your worth comes from. Worship God before, during, and after any ministry problem you face.

When kidmin leaders have the courage to run toward a problem, we begin to develop into the change agent God intended for us to become. When kidmin leaders do the work to get our ministry right instead of blaming our problems on others, we earn the right to then go toward church leadership to begin total church buy-in. Getting ministry right is about having extreme clarity, perspective, favor, and the ability to listen (not run!). When we lead with this humble posture, we will be likely to have the right to speak into and influence the grander vision of the church for God's glory.

Part 2

INFLUENCING THE GRANDER VISION OF YOUR CHURCH

You've scrubbed the floors, tidied the living room, prepared the meal . . . the house is in order! You are officially ready for the big party because you got your stuff together! Yes, it's kinda like that. Because you have helped others see what you see, you have placed yourself in a better position to influence the grander vision of your local church.

In chapters 4, 5, and 6, we will focus on you influencing the grander vision of your church moving forward. We will examine how being a student of your senior pastor and building strong partnerships with the other ministries in your church will strengthen your alignment to the grander vision of the church. You will ultimately improve your ability to implement ministry plans that are embedded in the core of your church mission.

As you seek to influence and drive change from your unique leadership role, we cannot emphasize enough how important this section of the book is. When moving through this section, pray that our creative, wise, and all-powerful God will give you fresh insight as you think through how to apply what you are reading. If you've been in ministry a while, it may be that these areas are important reminders more than they are new discoveries. But if you are relatively new to kidmin, learning these critical leadership skills now can dramatically increase the effectiveness of your leadership. The competencies discussed in this section are the essential ingredients that distinguish the most effective kidmin leaders who seek to influence and lead change within the local church.

4

Aligning to a Larger Vision

Your church publicly says that a core value is "reaching" those who don't know Christ, yet you see little fruit, activity, or even strategy direction . . . what should you do?

It was a beautiful March day in Orlando. My husband and I had already landed in Florida two days earlier to get the rented condo stocked with food, diapers, and anything else our kids and grandkids might need during their weeklong stay visiting our favorite mouse—Mickey!

After our daughter's family was all settled, we began scoping out which Disney parks we wanted to visit on what days. I remember our two granddaughters' joy-filled screams as we drove closer to the land of magic, Walt Disney World.

As we took in the sights, I found myself feeling like Walt himself—a kid at heart, as he has been described. Whitney Stewart, author of *Who Was Walt Disney?*,[1] describes Walt Disney's dream of wanting to create a place where families, not just kids, could go and have fun together. It would be like an amusement park with lots of rides, only cleaner, different, better!

WHAT CAN WE LEARN
FROM A MAN NAMED WALT?

Have you ever been there? I was amazed at the creativity, cleanliness, and unbelievable attention toward the guests of the Disney parks. Our granddaughter was walking through one area of the park wearing her princess attire. As we passed every hired park employee, each stopped and knelt down in front of our granddaughter to get the best eye contact possible. "Hello Princess! You look beautiful today. Is there anything I can get you to enjoy your day more?" We were stunned as we heard these words coming to our granddaughter from someone who didn't even know her! Imagine how excited she was when one park employee handed her a cold juice to allow "the princess" to become more comfortable on a hot day (with no cost to us!).

When our son and his family arrived the second week, we weren't sure we would get the same treatment, because this was known as one of the most crowded weeks of the year for the park—spring break. We packed our snacks and sunscreen, and off we went to their first park experience. As we approached the main entrance, we pulled up to the cashier booth to pay for parking. We were asked if we were here to celebrate anything special. I quickly responded, explaining we were celebrating being at Disney with our son and his family. "Great!" said the man at the gate. "Enjoy your day. The mouse paid for your parking today, so go right in!" Now, this was much better than a cold drink of juice to me!

We parked the car and headed in on the tram, enjoying our grandson's excitement as he was yelling hello to the wooden characters set up to mark the parking lot (for those of us who needed landmarks to remember parking locations—and that includes me!). At every turn and every park of Walt Disney World, we encountered the exact same treatment we experienced the week prior. The staff and the environment were just as excellent, working together to make sure everyone had the best experience possible.

Author Bill Scollon, who wrote *Walt Disney: Drawn from Imagination*, explains the reasoning behind what we experienced.

> Often, when on a business trip, Walt would visit zoos, fairs, circuses, carnivals, and amusement parks. He studied what made them appealing, which attractions pleased people the most, and what the overall experience was. Many parks were dirty, littered, badly maintained, and full of unfriendly workers. Walt knew there had to be a better way. . . . Even during construction, Walt would often tell the engineers to crouch down next to him and imagine how a building would look from a low angle. He wanted them to appreciate how a child would experience the park. . . . The park would be steeped in American traditions, history and experiences. Walt wanted kids and parents alike to come away having learned something new.[2]

Walt Disney created timeless core values that were handed down from one year to the next, one park to the next. Martin Gitlin, author of *Walt Disney: Entertainment Visionary*, explains these timeless core values in another way.

> A polite and courteous staff at Disneyland was very important to the man who created it. On one occasion, Disney and wife Lillian were about to enter an exhibit, but the guard at the entrance would not let them through. When Disney identified himself, the guard allowed him to pass, but refused entrance to Lillian, whom the guard did not know was his wife. Disney fired the guard on the spot. He then called the staff together and explained to them that all guests must be treated as if they were guests at his own home. . . . Disney was obsessed with keeping his theme park sparkling clean.[3]

Polite and courteous staff, better known as "cast members," would be onstage and part of the show displayed. Sparkling clean parks. Making sure every family member enjoyed themselves. Coming away with learning something new. Creating an interesting and fun environment for kids. These are Disney's great core values in action! These values have stood the test of time. They don't stifle creativity. They set up the foundation of what is most important. They bring chemistry. They bring focus. They bring loyalty to the brand. They bring unity and harmony. Without them, chaos can settle in.

MISALIGNMENT: ARE YOU OUT OF SYNC?

Webster's dictionary defines misalignment as *the incorrect arrangement or position of something in relation to something else.* If we had experienced misalignment within the Walt Disney parks, we would have felt a gap. What if, rather than juice and a smile, our little princess had been greeted with rude indifference by park employees? Now that would have been a misalignment in a destination proclaiming itself "The Happiest Place on Earth"!

Here's an example from the local church context. The staff or ministry team all agrees on a discipleship strategy, but one of the staff members doesn't cooperate in execution of the strategy. This misalignment is really frustrating to you. Do you close the gap with a candid conversation? Or walk away, still frustrated?

Your church publicly says that a core value is "reaching" those who don't know Christ, yet you see little fruit, activity, or even strategy direction. The misalignment between the "church messaging" and "what's actually happening" makes you uneasy. What should you do?

A new family in your church hears that your church wants them to have a "place to belong," yet when they arrive at a planned event, they feel unwelcome, and others at the event seem focused only on their own little clique. How does this family respond to this misalignment?

Our family experienced a gap that caused relational strife. When our daughter was a young girl, I remember her wanting to go to a friend's home for a Friday night sleepover. My husband and I had a core value of making sure we carved out multiple times each week to have uninterrupted family time. It just happened that Friday nights, when our kids were young, seemed to work as one of these family times of the week. It was our strategy in how we held up this core value.

As our daughter got older, most of her friends wanted to watch movies or just be together on Friday nights. When she asked us if she could go to a Friday night sleepover, our first reaction was to say no—it stood in the way of our family core values. We had a gap! We decided it was very important to hold on to Friday nights, but was it *really*?

As we were sharing this dilemma with a mentor couple, we began to discover my husband and I were aligned in our family-time core value but we were becoming misaligned with our daughter because we were holding tight to how we *practiced* this core value. Our mentor couple challenged us to think of creative new ways, new strategies, to uphold our values as our children became older. Because our children were changing, our strategy needed to change. To be clear, our core value didn't change, but the way we executed the core value needed modifying. If we had kept relying on our Friday nights as the primary expression of our family-time core value, we would have been upholding the strategy more than the value.

Even with adult children, this core value hasn't changed for us. It is timeless. However, the way, or the strategies, in which we accomplish this core value should never stop changing if we want chemistry, focus, loyalty, unity, and harmony among each person in our family.

This is a story of misalignment within my *family*. But we know this happens in our ministries as well. What happens when we make our kidmin strategies more important than the core values of our church? Or what happens when our kidmin values are incorrectly positioned in relation to our church's core values that are at the foundation of its grander vision? We experience misalignment, and the families within our ministries sense this as well. Church leadership will feel the tension that can create a wrong allocation of resources. And, as kidmin leaders, we can lose our leadership voice to make real change in our children's ministry and our church.

As a leader in your church, you need to assess and identify the areas where you are lacking alignment in your church. You have probably already identified some and can even think of a few as you are reading through this chapter. Write them down. Record them on your laptop or mobile device. Begin to ask others where they see alignment gaps or unnecessary overlaps and take note of them, prioritizing in order of importance.

THE PRICE OF MISALIGNMENT

Misalignment can show up in a variety of ways:

Unnecessary overlap: A mild case of ministry misalignment *could* mean that you have some areas of your ministry where you are duplicating (unnecessary overlap of) your time, effort, and resources, which translates into a mis-stewardship of resources and capacity. Let's take the way you inspire, equip, and engage parents in your kids ministry as an example. It may be that you have multiple areas of your children's ministry all trying to help parents engage with their kids spiritually, and parents are becoming overwhelmed. When you assess all of the channels your church is leveraging to equip parents (like events, take-home papers, online and email tools, weekend sermons, etc.) then you multiply that by the number of age-graded ministries, you may find that you are unnecessarily duplicating efforts.

Gaps: Misalignment not only shows up in the form of unnecessary overlap, but also in the form of gaps. A gap can be where we say one thing, but do another (maybe even unintentionally); therefore we do not live up to our promises (think Disney). One ministry friend of mine (Matt's) named Pete shared this story with me:

> When we looked at our ministry calendar and all that we asked families to do on the weekend we realized that we weren't living up to our own values. We value family, families worshiping together and honoring the Sabbath. However, we were asking families to attend Sunday worship together at one service, serve during the other, bring their middle-schooler to an afternoon program and their high-schooler back for an evening program. We were running parents ragged and undermining them and the Sabbath. There was no time to relax, to be together as a family, or to enjoy the Sabbath. So we decided to align our ministries to better serve the family and eliminate the gap between our values and our structure. Now all of our high school and middle school community groups meet on Wednesday evening at the same time as our children's ministry and we're so much more effective and fruitful because of it.

When misalignment shows itself in the form of a gap, our ministry effectiveness decreases. When an entire church vision is misaligned, the result can be chaos.

This often happens in a church where the different ministry teams (preschool, children, youth, etc.) are *not* held accountable to work to-gether toward a larger strategy, vision, or set of core values. A lack of accountability to the grander vision fosters chaos and can even impact your ministry culture. If you find yourself in this challenging situation, pray for your church leadership, and also consider reading Patrick Lencioni's book on organizational health titled *The Advantage.*[4] Needless to say, when church ministries enjoy a high level of alignment to the grander vision of the church, it's a sign of good health. The inverse could be said about low levels of alignment.

So, what if you see areas for improvement and growth in your ministry? Then it's time to recalibrate.

RECALIBRATING:
WHAT IT LOOKS LIKE IN YOUR CHURCH

Let's be clear: recalibration is a good thing. Think about it . . . your car's wheels get out of alignment, so you take them to the mechanic and he recalibrates them. Or life gets busy and your priorities get all out of whack . . . next thing you know your marriage or core relationships are out of alignment. So you sit down with your spouse and work hard to get back on the same page, rework your schedule, and reprioritize what's important to both of you. Recalibration is a common process we use across all areas of life to get us headed in the right direction.

But what does this process look like for you as the kidmin leader in the context of your local church?

Listen and learn, as we discussed in chapter 3. Being a lifetime learner and constantly listening is the first step. Stay humble and always invite others to speak into your ministry. Listen to what respected leaders have to say (leaders from both inside and outside your local church). Proverbs 15:22 says, "Without counsel plans fail, but with many advisers they succeed" (ESV).

Identify the areas of misalignment. We can identify these assessments in a number of ways: by making our own observations, making an assessment as a church leadership team, making the assessment as a children's ministry team, asking your top kidmin leaders and volunteers, asking parents for their feedback, and even engaging other respected leaders inside and outside of the ministry.

Partner with others to maximize effectiveness. Once we have identified and verified areas of misalignment, we have to work together with other teams, leaders, and key influencers to address them. We will discuss this in depth in chapter 6.

Author Jim Collins wrote an article for *The Forum* magazine in which he drives home the point that when we veer from our core values, misalignment takes place.[5] Collins challenges common thinking that it's all about the "vision statement." Certainly great vision statements are at the foundation of making great companies (or ministries). However, we tend to forget the importance of timeless, unchanging core values.

When we veer from our core values to accomplish our vision, we are essentially forfeiting our organizational DNA in exchange for a cheaper way of doing ministry. It can happen so easily if we are not careful (not just in kidmin, but in any area of the church). One example of this is when we forfeit relationships with kids (a likely core value in your children's ministry) in exchange for the convenience of weekend programming. The good news is that we *can* recalibrate to the grand vision (mission, vision, philosophy, values) of the church, but it will take your leadership to do it. If you were asked what is the vision of your church and how does it line up in your ministry, could you answer with clarity?

But again, as we've been saying—you can't recalibrate alone. You need a team around you.

WHEN WE'RE MISALIGNED
WITH GOD'S GRANDER VISION

God's grander vision for putting the world back together in Christ is found in the book of Ephesians. We read a description of the church and how the church is part of God's plan to reach the world, which is His grander vision. Ephesians reminds us Christ is the Head of the church and we are the body of His church. We are God's masterpieces, saved to serve Christ and to build up His church.

There was a man named Zechariah who had a deep desire to build God's church. Zechariah worked as a Jewish priest at the temple in Jerusalem. Zechariah was told before anyone else that God was setting in motion His grander vision of coming to Earth to begin putting the world back together.

One day, while on duty, Zechariah was chosen to be the priest who would enter the Holy Place to offer incense to God so the people would be reminded to pray when they saw the smoke from the burning incense. Suddenly he found himself face to face with an angel: "Don't be afraid, Zechariah! God has heard your prayer. Your wife, Elizabeth, will give you a son, and you are to name him John . . . And he will turn many Israelites to the Lord their God."[6]

This news was too much for Zechariah to understand and believe. Even though Zechariah had a core value that God could be trusted (read Luke 1:68–79), when the angel told him he and his wife were going to have a son in their old age, Zechariah began to doubt. *Zechariah lost his voice* because his level of faith did not align with God's grander vision.

Aaron, Moses's brother, *lost his credibility* with the Israelites as Moses was leading them toward God's grander vision of the Promised Land. God had a grander vision for the Israelites than what they were able to comprehend. Despite constant evidence of God's love and power, and His provisions for their physical and spiritual needs, the Israelites complained and yearned for their days in Egypt.

Even though Aaron and Moses made a good team, Aaron's life in following God was hot and cold. He gave into demands for a golden calf. He also joined his sister Miriam in complaining about Moses. Aaron lost his credibility because he yielded to public pressure instead of staying aligned with God's grander vision. His lack of credibility brought confusion to the life of the Israelites, which also limited his voice being heard.

Peter was given a platform to use his voice toward change. From studying Peter's life, we see he became the recognized leader among

Jesus' disciples, being called the "rock." We can also learn a very important life lesson from Peter's life. *It is better to be a follower who sometimes fails than one who fails to follow a leader* toward a grander vision.

At times in ministry, I have been just like Zechariah, Aaron, and Peter: a kidmin leader who has lost her voice and lost her credibility because her ministry was so far away from following and aligning with the grander vision of her church. At that time, I was more concerned with trying to stand firm on what I felt was right instead of standing on the timeless core values of our church. I should have been creating kidmin strategies that were aligned, compelling, winsome, and gripped the heart of church leadership, our volunteers, and our families. When I think back to those moments, I now realize I put church leadership in a sticky situation. Without being aligned, I wasn't playing my part in helping our church reach God's grander vision. Without being aligned and playing my part, why would church leadership have the desire to rightly allocate resources to my ministry? Have you been there? Or are you there now?

NOT JUST CHANGE, BUT CHANGE THAT ALIGNS TO THE GRANDER VISION OF THE CHURCH

Jim Collins makes a remarkable point about change: "Every institution—whether for-profit or not—has to wrestle with a vexing question: what should change and what should never change? It's a matter of distinguishing timeless core values from operating practices and cultural norms. Timeless core values should never change; operating practices and cultural norms should never stop changing."[7]

Change in your kids ministry is necessary, but the change must lead to greater alignment with the grander vision of the church in order for the change to be sustainable and effective. Let us share with you a courageous decision that Children's Pastor Randy Isola (Christ Community Church, St. Charles, Illinois) made recently:

For years, close to half the years our church has existed actually, our children's ministry had a mission statement that everyone gladly rallied behind. It was clear, concise and compelling. It was even biblical in the sense that it outlined a purpose clearly at the heart of the Gospel. Everything you would look for in a pithy nine-word summary of the overarching purpose behind all our children's ministries and programs. Yet over time I became increasingly dissatisfied with it.

It is my belief that as a children's pastor, one of my primary responsibilities is to take the vision God has given my senior pastor for our church and facilitate that vision being worked out in the children's ministry. So why would we want or need a separate vision statement? Our entire church is ultimately trying to accomplish the same purpose. Yes, there are a number of different age groups, various needs, and necessary ministries, but all with the same end in mind. So the mission statement of our children's ministry is now identical to the mission statement of our church. We now evaluate our entire ministry through the lens of our church's mission, which has led to some strategic changes in ministry planning and execution.

Jim Collins says that one way to identify your organization's timeless core values is by forming what he calls a Mars Group. This group consists of five to seven people who have a gut-level understanding of your organization, which allows them to recreate the very best attributes of your organization on another planet. Why is this so important? If they can't duplicate your organization (or ministry) in another place, then odds are increased you are confused about your core values to start with. This confusion will limit your grander vision from moving forward.

Who would you choose as your kidmin Mars Group? Would your Mars Group's core values and your church's core values be aligned?

For me (Pat) it all came together at a kidmin team gathering that we called Super Saturday! Super Saturday came the second Saturday morning of every month. It was a time for our leadership core to meet for strategy, prayer, and development. Since reading Collins's article, and wanting to gain my leadership voice and credibility, I asked the volunteers to bring a list of the top three to five timeless core values of our church and our ministry. I guess I looked at this team as my Mars Group! My dream was that both lists would align. Well, in our conversation . . . not so much.

Our Super Saturday "morning" became our Super Saturday "day." People didn't want to end the conversation because the more we talked and prayed, our gaps became amazingly clear. Let me give you an example.

At the top of both kidmin and the church's timeless core values list was the word "proximity." Our church and ministry would group people (adults and children) into small groups according to where they lived. But was proximity the real core value or was it a strategy? After an hour of discussion, we landed on it being a strategy, not our church or ministry timeless core value. We realized we had put so many policies and procedures in place for our families to follow to honor proximity that we had lost focus of the real core value. Families were starting to believe we cared more about where they lived than their child's spiritual growth.

We sat still and thought of the different small-group strategies our church had experienced—proximity, affinity, purpose, and so on. When we slowed down to think of personal experiences at our church and within our kids ministry, we drew a line through proximity on our list and wrote the words "authentic discipleship" in its place. Then, once we wrote "authentic discipleship" on our list of timeless core values, we were able to discern if this church-wide value was also seen within our children's ministry.

Today as I reminisce over the hard work we went through to become better aligned with our church, I have tasted the sweet chemistry with church leadership where my leadership voice is heard. Our volunteers are focused. We have unity and harmony. And I'm convinced our ministry is more effective.

Do you know the timeless core values of your church? Is your kids ministry aligned with these timeless core values—or not? If not, why, and what can you do?

I have kept these questions at the forefront of every ministry strategy conversation. If I want to be an agent of real change within our church through our kid ministry, I must make sure our ministry aligns with our church's timeless core values.

WHAT DOES THE RESEARCH TELL US?

IN OUR 2015 SURVEY we asked 340 kidmin decision makers, "To what degree does your children's ministry align with the larger vision of the church? Please answer using a 5-point scale where 1 is 'Not aligned at all' and 5 is 'Completely aligned.'" Pat and I were pleasantly encouraged that nearly one third of our participants (31.59%) rated this question at a "5—completely aligned." 39.01% responded by rating this a 4. And nearly one third (29.04) rated this a 3 or lower, indicating a lower level of alignment.

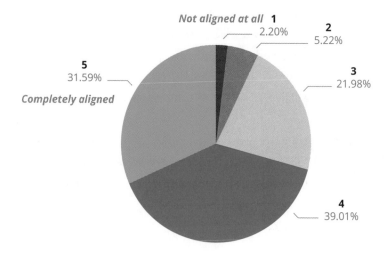

Not aligned at all **1** 2.20%

2 5.22%

5 31.59%
Completely aligned

3 21.98%

4 39.01%

We also asked, "To what degree does your vision for your children's ministry align with your senior pastor's desire for the children's ministry in the church? Please answer using a 5-point scale where 1 is 'Not aligned at all' and 5 is 'Completely aligned.'" Although the overwhelming response from this question was favorable, over one quarter (26.64%) rated this as a 3 or lower, indicating various levels of alignment challenges with the senior pastor's desire for the church.

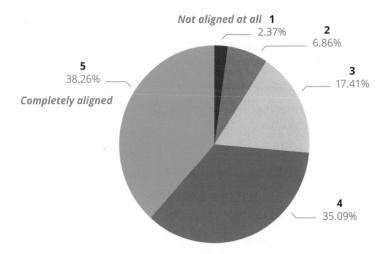

Here's where it gets really interesting. When asked, as a follow-up question with an "open" response, we received some very insightful feedback. The open-ended question was, "What obstacles do you think might be standing in the way of your children's ministry being more highly aligned with your senior pastor's desires?" Remember, just over one quarter (26.64%) indicated lower levels of alignment with the senior pastor's desire for the children's ministry. During this part of the survey, kidmin leaders like you were able to give us narrative or open feedback. After going back and coding each and every response, it became obvious that there are five major thematic challenges for those who are struggling with alignment, and they are as follows:

1. **Lack of time with my senior pastor (or another designated senior leader):** So many kidmin leaders want to have a close alignment with their senior pastor or senior leaders, but they simply do not *know* them or have enough time to achieve alignment. So many of those who struggle with greater alignment with their senior pastor or leaders seem to be crying out for more time to get to know and understand (as well as collaborate with) their senior leaders. We will explore this in depth in chapter 5.

2. **Lack of leadership above me:** Of those kidmin leaders who are struggling with wanting to attain greater alignment to their senior pastor's vision, this was the second most common response. Although it may not always be the senior pastor, according to a segment of kidmin leaders, someone above the kidmin leader on the staff org chart is not providing the much-needed clarity for the kidmin leader to know how to align.

3. **Lack of a clear vision from the senior pastor or leader:** As painful as this may be to report, the third most common response from those seeking greater alignment with the senior pastor's vision, was the single fact that the senior pastor didn't *have* a clear vision. Sometimes this was expressed in the form of a pastor who is not proficient and articulate in expressing the vision (which can be a competency issue). Other times it was expressed in an underdeveloped vision or even the lack of having thought through a vision for the church.

4. **Difference in philosophy:** Many frustrated kidmin leaders cited a difference in philosophy between the lead pastor and the kidmin leader. This was often expressed in the form of "my pastor doesn't see the value in children's ministry" or "my pastor doesn't see the value in working cross-functionally to reach and equip families."

5. **Communication:** Pat and I have forty-plus years of ministry experience, and we want to say, yet again, that you cannot work hard enough on being a better communicator . . . and this was very clear in the kidmin survey open responses as well.

These research findings and our personal kidmin stories can give us knowledge, but true wisdom comes when we have the ability to understand and act on that knowledge. In chapter 3, I (Pat) shared why I wanted to run from hearing feedback. If I had continued to run from the knowledge I received from our Super Saturday Day, I wouldn't be a wise kidmin leader making wise decisions.

Visionary leadership comes with big, God-sized dreams built on timeless core values aligned with God's grander vision for the church. And these are not formed in a vacuum—they are always being tested and refined in the iron-sharpens-iron interaction of our church community, as we've already seen. Let me share one more "alignment" story with you.

Following each service on a particular weekend, senior leadership asked our church members to stay afterwards for a church family meeting. As a kidmin leader, I have found that engaging in these gatherings can give me a great dose of reality and a better connection to the pulse of our church.

As the gathering turned from casting vision to a Q & A time, a man stood and asked a question that showed our ministry's gaps: "You just shared a compelling vision that authentic discipleship happens best in smaller communities where a person can be known, loved, and challenged. Why is it that my eight-year-old son is told his community group within our children's ministry has changed because he wasn't able to attend for the past few weeks?"

My face turned red and my heart raced as I wanted to defend our ministry. Senior leadership handled their response so beautifully by honoring the man's concern, and then asking him and other parents who faced the same gap to come down front at the end of this meeting.

I quickly moved down front, but as I reflect back over what I was truly thinking as I walked toward that conversation, I wanted to let it be known that this parent's son attended our children's ministry every three weeks at best! Of course we needed to create and uphold a policy based on small group attendance!

Well, this parent walked down and twelve additional parents followed him! You know what I learned? Defensiveness would only have made things worse. It would have shone a glaring spotlight on our ministry gaps . . . and on my inadequacies as a true change agent. As I chose an attitude of seeking to understand, I saw how I had been elevating our attendance policy to a core value—and it was out of sync with the grander vision of our church. And our parents saw it too.

The journey of becoming a true change agent will take honesty, submission, and conversations with church leadership and others to help us identify, name, and close the gaps we face.

5

How to Be a Student of Your Senior Pastor

How can you see your senior pastor as someone who can help you?

I (Matt) had just gotten off of a Google Hangout call with Amy, who was telling me about how well her church leadership team works together, when hardly a moment had passed and I got a text from Dave. Dave was expressing genuine concern about wanting to work more closely and more effectively with his lead pastor and senior leadership in his church. In a matter of minutes I was hearing deep expressions of the heart over the very same topic (the health and relationship between the kidmin leader and senior leadership) but from two very different perspectives. Why was it that Amy had such a growing and fruitful relationship with her senior leaders, but Dave was struggling?

What about you? Is your relationship with senior leadership vibrant and growing, filled with trust, favor, and open dialogue where you feel included in the grand vision of the church? Or is your relationship with the senior leadership of your church distant, stuck in a silo, even contentious?

No matter where you are in your relationship with your senior pastor (or senior leadership, depending upon the context of your church), this chapter aims to fertilize an ongoing, healthy relationship between kidmin leaders who already enjoy a positive relationship with senior leaders, as well as provide a foundation and starting place for those who are building from ground zero.

We realize that the readership of this book is coming from a broad set of local church contexts. Some readers may be part-time kidmin leaders who work closely with the senior pastor. Others may serve on a large staff and report to a senior leader other than the lead pastor. And everything in between! We've tried to take this into account and give you principles, strategies, and ideas that can be leveraged no matter the context as you apply them to your situation.

With that in mind, let's take a look at what we found in our research.

WHAT DOES THE RESEARCH TELL US?

WHEN PAT AND I conducted our 2015 research project, this particular area of learning was one of our top priorities. We really wanted to get to the bottom of how well we actually know our senior pastors. We asked the following five questions:

- **How well would you say you know the ministry heart of your senior pastor?**
- **To what degree are you a student (learning how to best serve, understand, and minister with) of your senior pastor?**
- **How often do you meet with your senior pastor?**
- **For what purpose do you meet with your senior pastor?**

- **Can you give examples of how you have been a student of your senior pastor?**

WE WERE VERY encouraged that the kidmin community reports that we know the ministry heart of our senior pastor, as over 75% of the respondents rated this question a 4 or a 5 (out of 5) or higher. However, when we asked, "To what degree are you a student of your senior pastor?" those who rated this a 5 or 4 fell to just over 62%, meaning that nearly 4 out of 10 children's ministry leaders are less engaged in getting to know how to best understand how to work with our lead pastors. As we sought to interpret the data, we began to think that many kidmin leaders may be less engaged in understanding the pastor's heart due to less accessibility. It was quite helpful to understand just how often we are meeting with our senior pastors.

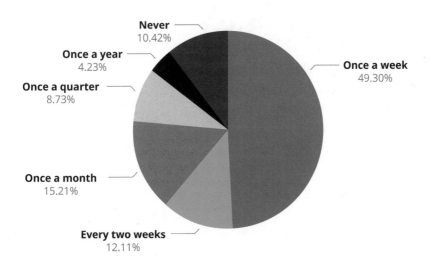

SIX OUT OF TEN kidmin leaders (healthy percentage) are meeting with their lead pastors once a week, gaining

*accessibility to and some level of personal relationship with their senior leader. On the flip side, nearly 4 out of 10 meet with their senior pastor once a month or less, and 1 out of 10 **never** meet with the senior pastor.*

What about those leaders who rarely meet with their senior staff? Lack of accessibility to the leader(s) who is (are) responsible for the primary vision and direction for the church puts you in a challenging spot when trying to best understand his heart and vision for the church.

Granted, every church staff model can be somewhat different. The larger the church staff, like at Willow Creek, the smaller the percentage of leaders who will have direct access to the senior leader.

WE ALSO asked kidmin leaders "For what purpose do you meet with your senior pastor?" To see the results to this question and for more access to the overall research project, go to Awana.org/ LeadingKidmin/Research for the free download.

But most importantly, *the leader who is responsible for the children's ministry needs some level of accessibility to either the lead pastor or the senior staff pastor who provides strategic direction and vision for the church.* Why? As a member of the overall church leadership team, in order to most effectively align to the grander vision of the church, you will need to build strong partnerships with the key leaders to fulfill the responsibilities of your ministry. It's incredibly difficult to know your leadership's ministry heart without some level of access to them.

Now, before you freak out, we realize you may be frustrated about now, thinking, "I rarely ever get to meet with my senior leader(s)! How will it ever change?" If this is where you're at, hang in there. We will equip you with a plan to improve this as we keep reading together.

I THOUGHT I KNEW WHAT WAS RIGHT

Twice a year, our church set aside a day when each ministry had the opportunity to choose people from their team to stand before church leadership and their peers from other ministry departments to share their next six-month goals and lessons learned from the previous six months. We called this day "Ministry Planning." After our stories were shared, ministry peers and church leadership had an opportunity to ask questions, challenge us, and then close with praying over the presenters and ministry. Weak knees or not, everyone knew the importance of this meeting. Everyone would make sure they came in prepared, rehearsed, and ready to go.

On this particular day, I (Pat) was partnered with another person from our team to share our children's ministry plan. Beforehand, we spent time crafting our message and deciding who would share what part of our story. Then, we both took the podium. But instead of our presentation going as planned, the person who was going to "stand with me" said "Pat is going to share our goals with you," and then walked off the stage!

I thought I was going to faint! Now what do I do? I timidly began speaking, finding myself breathing so fast that I was talking as if I just finished running a marathon! My lips even began to tingle! I remember tossing out a bold prayer to God: *Please, God, help me to breathe!*

When I finished and walked offstage no one really said anything, which was not normal. I felt so inferior that I was relieved nobody asked questions, not then and not later.

As I look back to that day, I now understand why I felt people were avoiding what had happened. I was a leader standing on the stage, obviously fearful, telling our ministry story. I usually came across to others as someone who could "handle" situations, but this time, the people around me didn't know how to respond. My fear and timid posture took them by surprise.

A few days later, I received a call from a church elder who was a great man with a huge heart. He shared that he heard what happened in our ministry plan presentation and wanted to see how I was feeling. My immediate thought was, "You heard about it? Who told you? What story did they tell you?"

Because I didn't take time to work through the emotions of that experience, instead of embracing his heart and intent behind calling me, I felt judged. He wasn't judging me. I was judging myself.

He continued, sharing he heard about what happened when he met with our senior pastor. When we ended our conversation I remember feeling embarrassed. I believed my leadership was now in question, and wondered what to do, if anything.

I decided to go for a short drive. My tears began as soon as I opened my car door. I went from sadness to fear to anger, back to sadness again. I begged God to help me in knowing what to do. Deep down, I wanted to bring some of my trusted coworkers on the ride with me so that I could get them on my side. You know, misery loves company. God gently showed me that pulling others into something like this would bring only dissension, not unity.

After more prayer and discussion with my husband, I knew my best next step was to ask for a meeting with our senior pastor. I had never done that before, but I put in a phone call to his assistant and found myself sitting with him an hour later.

After thanking him for the way he adjusted his schedule to meet with me that day, I told him I knew he talked with the elder, "probably sharing his concern about my leadership." As soon as I spoke those words, I saw him move his chair back a little. Was he going to get all defensive on me now? It didn't matter, because I now knew I was right because of the change in his body language. I saw the signs, so I judged him and went on with full force. I explained our presentation wasn't like we had rehearsed, and if he had a concern about my leadership why didn't he come to me instead of talking about it with someone else?

When I finished, he said something to me that I have never forgotten. "To make sure I understand, can I ask you some questions?" "Sure," I said. Then he said, "You feel I talked with others about your lack of leadership?" "Yes." "Are you wondering what I said or what I was thinking? Because your posture tells me you already made up your mind as to what I am thinking or what I did."

He asked me why I didn't start my ministry presentation with the truth. Something like, "Well, I can see how we planned to share our story with everyone has now changed. Can you give me a few moments to collect my thoughts?" I told him that would never cross my mind because that would make me and the ministry I loved so much look as if we were unraveling.

He leaned forward and with a tender look in his eyes he said, "Pat, without your vulnerability in that moment, you did unravel."

I knew he was right. As he continued talking, do you know what I learned? I learned the reason he had the conversation with the elder was not to talk about my leadership. It was for him to get counsel on how to change the environment of that gathering. He realized the environment wasn't pulling out the best from his leaders. It was causing stress, which only limits ministry moving forward.

It was through his grace and challenge that God showed me I was the one who judged him. In my fear and desire to protect myself and our ministry, I created a story in my mind that was not true.

Friends, if we are ever going to become a change agent from our kidmin leadership seats, we must move from judging our senior leaders to becoming a true student of them by wanting to do whatever it takes to seek to understand.

DOES YOUR ATTITUDE
OPEN DOORS—OR CLOSE DOORS?

In my journey that I've shared with you, I needed to do the hard work to make sure my actions and my heart were aligned. Gaining this understanding gave me three things. First, it gave me clarity to understand my shortcomings. Second, it gave me responsibility to take away any excuses and become accountable. Third, it opened doors for me to be a student of my senior pastor because this posture brought us both to a place of trust. Want to get through the door to your senior pastor's office (or another senior leader) to have a better relationship or healthier ministry? Consider what it takes.

Craig Groeschel, author and senior pastor of LifeChurch.tv, released a book titled *It*.[1] He describes "it" as something that is electric, an unmistakable camaraderie that cannot be faked. If you find your kidmin team or your relationship with your church leadership resembling different silos only passionate about their ministry area, you don't have "it."

Does your relationship with your senior pastor have "it"? When we enter our relationship with our senior pastor (or the executive pastor—whomever you report to) with a heart to serve and learn so that everyone wins, "it" takes root.

I decided it was time to see if I positively or negatively attracted "it" in my relationship with my senior pastor and other church leaders. This is what I wrote in my journal.

God, thank you for the way the conversation went today with Bill. I know he cares about the stories of how our ministry fits into our church's bigger picture. His desire, like mine, is for every person on my team to see how their role fits into our church's mission because we want our church to move forward in unity. Help me to continue to see the big picture.

Once again, today showed me the beauty of working through conflict. Thank you for the confidence I am learning in knowing how to respectfully say what is on my mind instead of talking behind closed doors with others. I really feel heard!

I am embarrassed to say, but I still find myself judging at times. When I get caught up in what I want for our ministry instead of our larger vision, I find I hold back and my heart begins to harden. God please forgive me. When my heart becomes hard, there is no way my relationship with my senior pastor (or anyone else for that matter) will grow. God, please help me to be a Philippians 2:1–4 type of person.

I need to lighten up! One of my strengths is responsibility. One of my downsides is responsibility. So many times when I am in a dark place, my strengths become my weakness. I want to grow in my relationship with my senior pastor by coming into that relationship with a sense of joy described in the book of Philippians. I want to stop depending on my circumstances and have joy in all circumstances. Joy will make relationships deeper and stronger.

Too many wins go without celebration. I want to grow in being on the lookout for excuses to celebrate my senior pastor, my team, and what God is doing through us as a team. God, help me to see them and celebrate them!

I had some work to do to bring "it." You may, too. Being a student of yourself and your senior pastor is at the foundation of making "it" happen. By having the right posture, and laying the groundwork for a good relationship with my lead pastor, doors opened for me to have a great working relationship with my pastor. Over the years, other kidmin leaders have taken note of this, especially since Pastor Bill Hybels is such a high-profile leader—so I often receive these three questions:

1. How can I be a better student of my senior pastor and better prepare for when we meet?
2. What do I need to do to gain access to my senior leader?
3. How should I use my time when I'm with my senior pastor?

I'll spend the next three sections walking you through these very important areas that will help you open doors with your senior pastor or other senior leaders on your church leadership team.

BEFORE I APPROACH THE DOOR: TIPS FOR BEING A BETTER STUDENT OF MY SENIOR PASTOR

Opening doors is about grace, seeking understanding, and gaining wisdom. That has been the lens I put my agenda through before entering any conversation with senior leadership. I remember a time when budgets were being allocated. I received our kidmin budget hours before meeting with Bill. I was frustrated because I didn't understand why some line items got cut, but bringing that frustration into our conversation wouldn't help move anything forward. So, I began by thanking him for the gracious heart of our church and shared how I know our ministry and the budget we receive is all God's, not mine. I confessed my previous attitude and then asked him this question: What process do you go through when deciding on financial allocations to different ministry needs? How can I do this better within our kidmin area?

That posture allowed us to view each other with grace. I learned his thinking and wisdom as I posed the question for him to speak into it. Before approaching the door, if you want to be a better student of your senior leadership, remember grace, seeking understanding, and gaining wisdom.

IN OUR RESEARCH we asked the question, "Can you give examples of how you have been a student of your senior pastor?" There were almost three hundred open-ended responses, but below is a short list of our favorites:

- By asking formative questions to align the ministry to overall church mission and vision.
- I occasionally ask him what books he's reading, and I go and read the same books. Then I'll follow up and ask him a question or two about what he thought was most significant about the book.
- I regularly ask my senior leader for feedback and apply the changes that make the most sense.
- Listening to my pastor's weekend sermons even if I have to listen to them online (because I'm serving in children's ministry at that time).
- When my pastor speaks and shares his vision, I listen very carefully and take notes.
- I asked what his personality style and top strengths were and made notes of what I learned to help me best approach and understand him.
- I pay close attention to how he manages difficult situations.
- I regularly ask him for his advice and wisdom.
- I go to my senior pastor before we implement anything big. We invite him into the discussions at the beginning of any major decision or project. Sometimes he doesn't have many concerns, but I've earned his respect by coming to him on the front end of the major initiatives.

- I intentionally ask questions, such as "what are your thoughts about . . ." or "this is how we've done it in the past; does it match what you feel is important?"
- I pray for him and his family regularly.
- I try hard to recognize and understand the "why" behind what he does.
- I have asked him whom he looks to for leadership and guidance. I've asked him what books he's reading and what other churches he respects so I can get an understanding of a ministry he appreciates.

Wow! What an encouraging list of ideas. So much we can learn and apply immediately! Now that we have some ideas on how to be a student of our senior pastor, let's move toward what we can do to gain the needed access to our senior leader (this isn't a challenge for everyone, but as we discovered earlier, nearly four out of ten kidmin leaders meet with their senior leader only once a month or less).

GETTING TO THE DOOR: HOW CAN I GAIN ACCESS TO MY SENIOR PASTOR?

If you are one of the fortunate kidmin leaders who have consistent times with your senior pastor, thank them! If you find yourself struggling to get to the door, think of what Darren, a kidmin leader, did at his local church. He made sure he sent more encouragement to his senior pastor than he did requests to get into his office. He chose to view his relationship with his pastor as "equity." He regularly asked himself, "How much equity do I have with my senior leader?" If he had taken more withdrawals from the relationship than he had been making deposits, then Darren knew it was time to invest more in the relationship and build up that equity.

Darren shared that once his senior pastor knew his heart was "for him and the bigger vision of the church," then when he did request a time to meet, not only did he come in very well prepared, but he was given the time needed to help move ministry forward from his kidmin seat. If we are not careful, we can inadvertently communicate that we only come to our senior leaders when we have needs (withdrawals). Darren showed that he was a proven ministry partner.

Does your senior pastor view you as a "ministry partner"? What about a team player? Our experience tells us that if you take on the leadership posture of becoming a ministry partner and a team player (not just an employee), then you will raise the equity in your relationship with your senior leader(s). This investment will help you gain greater favor with your senior pastor.

Pat and I (Matt) have a kidmin friend named Steve who ministers in a church culture where his conversations with senior leadership happen more organically: hallway conversations, pop-in meetings, and weekly gatherings (both formal and informal). But not every leader has this luxury. If you don't have day-in, day-out access to your lead pastor, you may need to think like Donna and schedule ahead.

Donna has a regular once-a-month meeting with her senior pastor. She honors these meetings and when she does have them, she stewards them responsibly. She shared a recent email to the pastor's assistant with me where she says, *"Hey Patti! I know I just met with Pastor Dan a week and a half ago, but I have one item where I need to engage him in some strategic discussion and another item I'd like him to help me make a decision on. I can make it quick. Probably 15–20 minutes. Can you help us find a time slot in the next few days? Thank you!"*

Notice Donna's tone and professionalism. This is an effective little piece of communication.

ONCE I'VE WALKED THROUGH
THE DOOR, WHAT DO I NEED TO KNOW?

Agatha, wanting to do more than coordinate her children's ministry, shared she would make sure she came in with a shorter agenda than what she wanted to have so she wouldn't bombard her senior pastor with one thing after another. She called it her critical list.

It's important when meeting with your senior pastor to be prepared, like Agatha. Have an overall objective for your time together. Make sure you come into this meeting organized as a way of showing honor and respect. This means that you need your discussion points and/or questions lined out in an orderly fashion (your critical list). Having a typed-up "agenda" of what you want to discuss is a common best practice (either on your mobile device or a printed piece of paper). If you begin to sense that your leader's attention is waning, then cut to the chase and only tackle the most important topics, and delay the leftover items for another gathering.

> **When I enter into a meeting with my senior pastor, I want to always make sure I come in prayed up.**

Juan mentioned he knew his senior pastor was known to move very fast in his thinking and was more of a visual learner than an auditory learner. To help his senior pastor stay focused, Juan would have one sheet with a visual explanation of the agenda item and his questions listed. What Juan taught me was to be a true professional. A true professional knows and understands how others learn, and adapts the way they communicate to their audience. Does a missionary to a French-speaking country go in speaking German, expecting the people to understand another language? It's the job of the communicator to adapt their communication style to their audience to be sure the message is clearly understood. Through my friendship with Juan I learned to be a true professional by taking the attitude that "it's my job to adapt my communication style to speak the language of my senior pastor" . . . not the other way around.

Most succinctly and most importantly, when I enter into a meeting with my senior pastor (or other senior leaders), I want to always make sure I come in prayed up. My senior leaders need my prayers and the prayers of others, and there is no better time to pray then when preparing for our time together.

WHAT IF I HAVE A CONCERN ABOUT MY SENIOR PASTOR?

First and foremost, believe the best until having the facts to prove otherwise. In Matthew 7:1–6, Jesus forbids us to judge others until we have done two things. First, Jesus wants us to take responsibility for anything we did to contribute to the problem. Second, He wants us to see clearly and understand the motives or intentions of what someone else has done.

Assuming facts, speculating motives, or jumping to conclusions is exactly what I did before and during the meeting with my senior pastor earlier in the chapter. I wasn't following Jesus' direction, but my senior pastor was. He believed the best in me and he searched for any facts that told him differently. God calls us to withhold judgment and look for a reasonable explanation. He calls us to never judge a book by its cover. He calls us to be a student of our senior pastor, not one who judges them.

Senior leaders are human. We are all sinners, needing God's grace. If you have deeper concerns about your pastor, even after going through all the proper channels, or you feel you are in a toxic situation, make sure you follow a modified Matthew 18 strategy, keeping your thoughts (and tongue) in check so you don't find yourself in a gossip situation. First, talk with your senior pastor. Second, if that doesn't go well, explain (not threaten) you did not feel heard. Explain it is time to bring in an objective party you both feel comfortable with to help your relationship get reconciled.

Only you will know if you need to have an exit strategy. Please, don't run. Don't gossip. Don't cause dissension. Ask God for guidance.

GAINING AND KEEPING TRUST

Trust has taken a hit in many facets of our life. We have trust issues in our relationships, our politicians, the economy, the media, other institutions . . . Should I go on? Trust in a relationship is a gift and it is a critical link for you to strengthen your relationship with your senior pastor.

Trust brings us hope and health. It helps us place our confidence in a person, place, or thing. After studying the life of Joseph found in the book of Genesis, we learn trust takes time to build.

From Exodus 16:2–3, we learn that lack of trust leads to cynicism, withdrawal, doubt, and stress as we read of how the Israelites came to not trust in Moses and Aaron. They began to speak bitterly against them.

Moses speaks of how trust is broken by unkept promises in Numbers 30:1–2: "Moses spoke to the heads of the tribes of the people of Israel, saying, 'This is what the Lord has commanded. If a man vows a vow to the Lord, or swears an oath to bind himself by a pledge, he shall not break his word. He shall do according to all that proceeds out of his mouth'" (ESV).

Moses reminds us the promises we make to God and others must be kept. In the time of this Scripture, people didn't sign written contracts. Their word was a binding signature. Breaking a vow, your word, meant broken trust, leading to a broken relationship. Trust is still the basis of our relationship with God and others. A broken promise today is just as harmful as it was in Moses's day.

Proverbs 26:25–26 speaks of how our actions show our true colors. "They pretend to be kind, but don't believe them. Their hearts are full of many evils. While their hatred may be concealed by trickery, their wrongdoing will be exposed in public."

After thinking through my relationship with my senior pastor, I have identified questions I had to honestly answer to take responsibility for growing our trust. Questions like . . .

- Do I act with integrity in a consistent manner that reassures my senior pastor I can be relied upon?
- Am I being transparent and honest with people at all levels of our organization?
- Am I accountable for my actions?
- Do I follow through?
- Am I open to feedback?
- Do I tell it straight, being open and honest about bad news, or do I spin the story?
- Do I resolve concerns head-on?
- Do I admit mistakes?
- Am I responsive to the needs of others?
- Am I looking to make sure everyone wins?
- Am I a walking example of what our church believes?
- Am I taking credit for someone else's work?
- How do I react when I am told "no"?
- How do I handle power?

Is there any encouragement from belonging to Christ? Any comfort from his love? Any fellowship together in the Spirit? Are your hearts tender and compassionate? Then make me truly happy by agreeing wholeheartedly with each other, loving one another, and working together with one mind and purpose. Don't be selfish; don't try to impress others. Be humble, thinking of others as better than yourselves.

> *Don't look out only for your own interests, but take an interest in others, too.*[2]

These words from Paul sum up the beauty of trust and how we must go about building it in our relationships. Walking into every conversation with my senior pastor with an open heart and mind; assuming the best and seeking to understand his behavior; and showing my true colors in our relationship will build trust, which opens doors for me to be a change agent from my kidmin leadership seat. Are your intentions clear or foggy with your senior pastor?

Being a student of your senior pastor will require you to keep an open mind. It will require your senior pastor to grow in trust with you as they see your trust in action more than they hear about it. It will require you to do what it takes to have "it" in your relationship—to see your senior pastor as a qualified person to help you make decisions and to have a united front in creating the action steps needed to reach the end together. The outcome? Honoring God through being a true example of humility.

6

Building Partnerships That Work

More than any other finding in our research, kidmin leaders told us that local churches are struggling with collaborating within the church.

Would you like to guess what the #1 pain point was in the 2015 research project we conducted?

Ask Kelly. Because she's been feeling the pain. After years of trying to partner with others in her church's children and youth ministry, Kelly informed me (Matt) that she was very discouraged. Kelly works on a church leadership team as a full-time kidmin leader. Their church's children's ministry, youth ministry, and adult ministry staff is composed of full-time leaders, part-time leaders, and some committed volunteer directors. One day she confided in me and said, "Matt, we have really great people on our staff. We are committed to the vision, have good team camaraderie, we read the same books, even attend some of the same conferences, but we just can't seem to execute what we give lip service to. It's like we agree on a common strategy, but we can't seem to partner together to pull it off. It's discouraging."

Have you ever felt like Kelly? This is a common frustration for those in kids ministry—all too common, according to our research. *More than any other finding in our research, kidmin leaders told us that local churches are struggling with strategizing and collaborating with other partners in the local church.* What made this particular item in our research so obviously painful was the massive gap between how highly we say we recognize the need to "strategize, collaborate, and lead cross-functionally" as compared with how well we are actually attaining this.

WHAT DOES THE RESEARCH TELL US?

IN OUR RESEARCH, when kidmin leaders were asked, "To what degree do you sense a need to strategize, collaborate, and lead cross-functionally (example: children's ministry team working with the youth ministry team) with other parts of your church ministry?" 88.04% rated this a 4 or a 5. Obviously, this is a huge recognized need by the kidmin community. However, when asked, "How well is your church leadership actually strategizing, collaborating, and leading cross-functionally?" 65.49% rated this only a 3, 2, or a 1. That's over 6 out of 10 kidmin leaders who are experiencing varying degrees of frustration or failure!

"How well is your church leadership actually strategizing, collaborating, and leading cross-functionally? Please answer using a 5-point scale where 1 is "Very poorly" and 5 is "Very well."

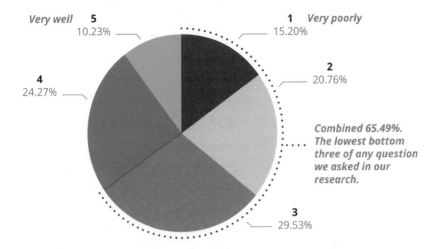

To be clear, over 6 out of 10 kidmin leaders are saying that local church leaders are struggling with strategizing and collaborating cross-functionally.

SEEING THIS NUMBER, in black ink, in our quantitative research only validates what Pat and I know to be true of our anecdotal experience and engagement with local church kidmin leaders. Some common complaints sound something like, "I would love to work more collaboratively, but our youth pastor operates in a silo" or "I don't seem to have what it takes to pull the youth ministry team together with the kidmin team" or "I've tried to work collaboratively, but no one on staff seems to be interested" or "If I could just help my senior pastor see what we are dealing with" or "Our elders are just not interested in children's ministry."

LEADING: DOWNWARD, UPWARD, LATERALLY

So many of us can relate to the above comments. But can I share a secret with you? It. Starts. With. You.

A friend of mine once told me (Matt), "If you want a friend, be a friend." My wife and I tell our two sons on a regular basis, "Model the very behavior you expect out of others. Lead by example, even if it takes others a long time to catch on."

Friends, this is hard work. It's gritty. But today's kidmin leader who wants to solve systemic problems in the church needs to be committed to digging deep, leading downward, leading laterally, leading upward, and modeling the kind of collaborative behavior (laying the foundation for building partnerships) and attitude you expect from others, even if in the beginning, you are the only one who is doing it. Let us give you some practical tips on how to win over those key partnerships you need to drive change from the kidmin seat.

LETTING YOURSELF BE INFLUENCED

If you want to influence others, you have to first let yourself *be* influenced.

Several years ago, God brought me (Pat) to the realization it was time to leave my role as Willow's weekend children's ministry director and transition to become our church's marriage director. Wanting to make a larger impact in the families within our church, I shared this new vision with some trusted friends. They understood the idea that impacting a marriage would change the heart of a home, which in turn would be the best place for a child to experience God's love. They knew how my husband and I wanted to use the story of our marriage to bring hope to other couples. But when it came to them affirming me in this new role, they just didn't get it.

I had no previous schooling in marriage counseling. I had no relationships built with those serving in this ministry. Their doubt caused me to doubt. But I sensed that God called me to this new adventure. I believed He would show me the way.

As kidmin leaders, it can be tempting to go it alone. It's all on you.

He did on a Tuesday morning in June. I found myself reading the book of Mark. "But you must really believe it will happen and have no doubt in your heart. I tell you, you can pray for anything, and if you believe that you've received it, it will be yours. But when you are praying, first forgive anyone you are holding a grudge against, so that your Father in heaven will forgive your sins, too."[1]

I knew I "first needed to forgive" my friends for their doubt. And to be forgiven.

After taking steps in asking God and my friends for forgiveness, I was ready to ask God for what I needed to lead the marriage ministry. I needed a mentor. So, instead of isolating myself, I asked God for the wisdom to know who to ask and the courage to ask each person He brought to mind. Within two weeks I had three mentors! One mentor is a theologian and a founder of our church; one mentor is a marriage and family counselor; and the third mentor was a key marriage ministry volunteer. To this day these three mentors walk with me.

As kidmin leaders, it can be tempting to go it alone. You may be *the* person in your church who deals with children's ministry. It's all on you. But is there someone in your church or in your circle—a seasoned ministry leader; a dear, wise friend who knows you well; a professional in the field—who could become your influencer? Without a real effort in being open toward others' thinking, we are shutting the doors to building healthy partnerships.

LITTLE EFFORT, LITTLE RESULT

I (Pat) enjoy keeping my eye out for quotes that I could make into little reminders I place in my office. Here are three for you:

"If you kinda sorta try, then you'll kinda sorta get results."
—Anonymous

Another one is, "The results you achieve will be in direct proportion to the effort you apply." —Denis Waitley, motivational speaker

And finally, the African proverb that says, "If you want to run fast, run alone; if you want to run far, run together."

Together. It is up to you to become a relentless kidmin leader who is on a mission to change the status quo of the relationships you have with other influential people in your church. Little effort in building these healthy partnerships will limit your influence. Remember the encounter between Moses and his father-in-law, Jethro, in the book of Exodus where Jethro challenged Moses's thinking around building an effective leadership structure? If you've not read this section of Scripture, you *gotta* go and check it out (it's found in Exodus 18).

Essentially, Jethro said a very hard thing to Moses, but it was something Moses needed to hear. He said something like, "Moses, son, you're killin' yourself! You're gonna burn out, bro. How do you expect to last as a leader if you don't surround yourself with other reliable leaders who can take some weight off of you and help you increase and expand your effectiveness? Let me show you how you can fix this by building partnerships . . ." Then Jethro proceeded to draw an org chart in the proverbial sand. The day that Jethro took Moses to leadership school and discussed the importance and value of partnerships was a game changer for Moses.

Let me give another example. It was springtime, when all kidmin leaders are wondering how they are going to recruit volunteers to serve during the summer to give their regular, dedicated weekly volunteers a well-deserved rest. I remember feeling I had exhausted every marketing idea so far, and we were still short volunteers for the upcoming summer. Then, God brought an idea to me that changed everything!

He began to show me how I needed to join forces with another ministry area. I sat on this thought for a few weeks and then had an "aha" moment (more on that in the next chapter!). Our church's small group ministry department had a deep desire to help people grow spiritually through serving. What if I bolstered *their* desire for people to grow through service by making *our* summer kids ministry that opportunity?

So I asked the small group ministry leaders to join me. I began by asking them their dreams and desires for their groups this summer. I learned they wanted discipleship to continue primarily by increasing the group's sense of community through them serving together. I then pitched a simple, realistic, cost-effective, quick-to-adopt, and fast-to-implement strategy for both of us! I explained we would keep their groups together by arranging for a group to serve in one age/grade level, *and* I would arrange a "group connection celebration" following each service so that these ministry leaders would have a platform with the groups. We would make sure the group stayed together. The small group leaders loved the idea! It was a definite win/win for sure!

That year saw our best summer recruitment because I leveraged relationships within the church in a way that solved a problem for each of our teams. I moved our recruitment strategy from recruiting individuals to recruiting a group of people. And we were able to recruit 30 percent of those groups serving during the summer to continue their service and become part of our children's ministry family!

Think of your ministry. What dream has God been placing on your heart that He wants you to move forward? What other ministry partnerships do you need to build so that this dream becomes a reality? If you (and/or your team) need to spend more time discerning whom to partner with and how to grow these partnerships, feel free to use the bonus material in the "Now It's Your Turn" discussion guide in the back of the book.

BE RELENTLESS TO FINISH THE RACE TOGETHER

When Ron Hunter and I (Matt) set out to launch the D6 Conference, we knew it was not a sprint but a long-distance run. We had just enough sense to know we couldn't do it alone. In those early days, when D6 was more of a conversation than it was a conference, it all started with partnerships. To this day, when I think back on that time period, and the momentum that grew so quickly, much of that momentum can be attributed to three very strategic partnerships with Christian leaders whom many of you would know by name if I mentioned them.

God knew we needed these partnerships as catalytic accelerants to advance the family ministry conversation through the D6 platform. Because of the partnerships that we invested in heavily we were connected to anyone and everyone we needed connecting to . . . sort of like walking backstage at the Willow Creek Leadership Summit and saying, "I'm with Bill." We just got in. We could not have attained that on our own. *We ran farther, because we had the right partners.*

The book of Hebrews speaks directly to how God wants us to run our ministry race. "Therefore, since we are surrounded by such a huge crowd of witnesses to the life of faith, let us strip off every weight that slows us down, especially the sin that so easily hinders our progress. And let us run with endurance the race that God has set before us. We do this by keeping our eyes on Jesus, the champion who initiates and perfects our faith."[2]

There have been many kidmin leaders before us who worked tirelessly to impact kids for Christ and develop spiritual champions. And there will be many after us. But if we are going to run our race with influence and impact, we need to follow what we are told in the above verses. Are we running the race that God has set before us or is it our race? Who are your eyes on from start to finish?

"No discipline is enjoyable while it is happening—it's painful! But afterward there will be a peaceful harvest of right living for those who are trained in this way."[3]

Putting in the effort needed to build healthy partnerships and effect change will come with pain. But we can tell you from our experience, it is all worth it!

"Look after each other so that none of you fails to receive the grace of God. Watch out that no poisonous root of bitterness grows up to trouble you, corrupting many."[4]

And if someone we are trying to partner with doesn't see the vision as quickly as we would hope, we cannot allow disappointment to turn into resentment. God wants us to finish the race well. He will bring you His favor.

Let us finish the race together!

NINE STEPS TOWARD HEALTHY PARTNERSHIPS

HERE ARE THE TOP NINE action steps I continue to use today to build partnerships:

ACTION STEP #1: Keep an open face—It is so easy to show the stress or conflict that might arise within us as we are in conversations with other ministries that will challenge one's thinking. When many people face stress or conflict, they often show this discomfort by "closing" their face. They might frown, close their eyebrows together, clench their jaws—you know, they just show a closed face instead of an open one.

ACTION STEP #2: Listen on purpose—*Problems will arise as you try to build these partnerships. One way to limit any relational problem is for you, as the kidmin leader who wants to influence change, to truly hear the other's concerns and thoughts. Try not to nix their ideas before hearing them out. Slow down and listen instead of planning your reply before they finish talking.*

ACTION STEP #3: Use "we" instead of "you" or "I"—*Remember, you are developing a unique team that will increase your influence and impact. Be cooperative, not competitive or self-seeking.*

ACTION STEP #4: Have a bias toward "yes"—*Try to be open to what God might be doing through others for impact. When we move into a conversation with our minds made up, we can find ourselves walking away thinking they are not being a team player, but in reality, it is you and I who are not because we forgot our bias toward "yes."*

ACTION STEP #5: Help them help you—*I have found sometimes I need to creatively think how to help those I am partnering with to connect the dots. It is our responsibility to guide them to see the big picture. Share the macro vision before the micro details. Help reduce any fuzziness by sharing compelling stories rather than giving a presentation.*

ACTION STEP #6: Revisit your church's mission often—*Every person in every role of your church needs to understand how their role is critical in accomplishing your church's mission. Without it, people wander and often choose to leave ministry. When you keep your church's mission at the forefront of your mind in every partnership, everyone wins.*

ACTION STEP #7: Express your desires, not your demands—*You want people to leave your conversations with energy toward the end goal. When you come with demands, that will shut down their creative thinking and impact will stop. When you express your desires and listen for theirs, then a great solution will develop.*

ACTION STEP #8: Show respect—*I think this one is self-explanatory!*

ACTION STEP #9: Run with them and be a part of the solution—*The energy brought between people running together brings a better possibility of finishing a race. Run with your ministry partnerships. When a problem arises, be the first person to let go of your agenda to creatively find a solution that will be a win for everyone. Sometimes the solution might be for you to let go of one of your desires. Remember, the reason you are taking these action steps is to increase your influence and impact. Letting go can show you are more about the church's mission than your own agenda.*

THESE ACTION STEPS will help your team become more cohesive. As this happens, you will have the greatest private influence because people will understand you as a loyal, trustworthy ministry partner. Andy Stanley has a great quote that sums up this section. "Public loyalty buys you private leverage." Amen!

Part 3

LEADING FROM WITHIN

Chapters 7, 8, and 9 focus on . . . you. Your actions, words, and approach to people and things have a big effect on those around you—a positive or negative effect. You want to change things . . . but does God want to change you?

As you read through the next three chapters, remember the first time you felt God's whisper and affirmation to become a kidmin leader. God wants to use you to do great things. He began a good work in you and will be faithful to complete it.

7

Listening to Those "Aha" Moments

These moments are catalytic. They are defining. And as kidmin leaders, we have an unlimited supply of those moments.

Some of us get flashes of insight in the shower: *this is what I should do!* Others of us, wrestling with a problem involving our career, our kid, our church, might be sitting at our laptop or out working in the yard when the moment comes. Alexander Graham Bell, discovering that the new machine he had been tinkering with for years actually worked, summoned his assistant: "Watson, come in here!" And some, as they are praying or reading God's Word, can feel almost a jolt: God is sending me a message!

We all experience these "aha" moments. These moments can make you laugh, cry, shout, pull you into a solution. "Aha" moments can inspire you to make a change because it is through them something is suddenly seen, found, or understood. Through them we can become unstuck. Kidmin leaders can experience these moments on a regular basis. We find ourselves solving a volunteer problem we've been stuck on, or we move away from previously planned lessons because we want the fog to clear and light bulbs to go on as we are teaching kids about God's larger story for their lives.

A children's ministry leader who seeks to drive real change within the local church is one who pays close attention to an "aha" moment, covering it with prayer and seeking discernment from the Lord.

THE SURGE IN THE BRAIN

Sitting in the doctor's office waiting to be seen, I (Pat) was reading a magazine to pass the time. I couldn't tell you what the article was about, but I can tell you all of a sudden I felt an urge to write down an idea on how we could engage high-school students to want to serve in our ministry! I couldn't find my pen fast enough! Before I finished writing my thoughts, the nurse came out to tell me my doctor was ready to see me. I grabbed my paper and pen, and not wanting to lose the idea, I kept writing as I was walking toward the examination room.

When my doctor came in, she saw the scribble on the paper. She asked me if they were questions that I wanted to ask her. I told her if she had the answer to this question, she would be a great speaker at a Next Gen conference! I told her, "I have been thinking about a particular question for a while and I never thought I would suddenly have an idea that could solve it sitting in your waiting room." My doctor began to explain the reasoning behind my light-bulb moment!

What she said next sounded a little like Doc Brown from *Back to the Future*: "Researchers say 'aha' moments are marked by a surge of electrical activity in the brain. People feel stuck before insight strikes. More times than not, they can't explain how they solved the problem and might say they are not even thinking about it, but they really are at an unconscious level. The solution appears suddenly and is immediately seen as being right." Great Scott! Those of us who believe God is the giver of the "aha" moments would praise Him for His creativity!

"NOW I GET IT"

As I drove home, I found myself revisiting her explanation. Then I was reminded about a team meeting that I was a part of earlier that day.

Our children's, student, and young adult leaders gathered to dig deeper into understanding the topic of divorce. We found we were having more conversations with those attending our ministries about the difficulty these young people feel of being caught between their mom and their dad. We believed we could do better when it came to knowing how to really meet them where they were, emotionally and spiritually. So we invited an expert to help us find our "aha" moments, so we could change how we were walking the hard journey of divorce with our kids and students.

We were watching a documentary on small children, teens, and adult children talking about the "other side" of experiencing divorce. The beginning of the video began with a stress reliever. We watched cute kids doing silly things with Mom or Dad as a couple; then, all of a sudden, we saw the same kids doing the same activities with their individual parent.

The video took a sharp turn as children, teens, and adult children began talking about their loss of identity. Story after story helped us realize one's personhood becomes shattered following the end of their parents' marriage.

When the video finished, you could hear a pin drop. Not being a child of divorce, I found my eyes full of tears thinking of the turmoil some kids in our ministry were feeling. Sitting with the new realization that kids are not as "resilient" as the culture tells us, I found myself praying for them by name. Then I began looking at the other team members in the room. Some remained still, wondering what to do or say. Others were trying to hold back their emotions as they relived the ache of that reality in their own stories.

Brad, one of our team members, stood up, his face showing anger and sadness. He had an "aha" moment, finally understanding why his adult children have decided to live in different states. "Now I get it. They moved to get away from the negotiation they would have to do on a daily basis with their mom and me since we still live in the same town." He then began to weep.

Brad had a painful "aha" moment—but it was this moment that gave him the strength to have the right conversation with his kids.

"Aha" moments are catalytic. They are defining. They bring us real wisdom. They can change the course of action. They never stop coming if you are one who has a hunger to learn and grow. They can be what God uses to redirect your life to bring you peace in knowing what He intends for you today. They bring growth, wisdom, and dreams. They are true turning points in learning.

As kidmin leaders, we have an unlimited supply of these moments. Those of us who decide to embrace our "aha" moments are those I would describe as a resilient community of leaders. They have the ability to maintain their ministry's core purpose and integrity among unforeseen shocks and surprises. They have the belief they can influence their surroundings and know there are valuable lessons in "aha" moments that will lead to learning, growth, and open the doors for them to become a change agent within their church. They develop grit as they persevere with passion and courage. "Aha" moments inspire Kidmin Leader change agents!

"WHEN HE FINALLY CAME TO HIS SENSES . . . "

It doesn't take us too long to search Scripture to find truth about "aha" moments. Kyle Idleman, author of a book titled, appropriately, *Aha,* defines such a moment as what happens when a sudden revelation surprises us with insight.[1]

We learn from Genesis 3, verse 7, that Adam and Eve's eyes were open at the very moment Adam took a bite of the fruit Eve already ate.

What did they do? *At that moment, their **eyes were opened**, and they suddenly felt shame at their nakedness. So they sewed fig leaves together to cover themselves* (emphasis added). Adam and Eve experienced the pain of their "aha" moment.

In the New Testament, Matthew reminds us of the "aha" moment Peter had.

When Jesus came to the region of Caesarea Philippi, he asked his disciples, "Who do people say that the Son of Man is?"

"Well," they replied, "some say John the Baptist, some say Elijah, and others say Jeremiah or one of the other prophets."

Then he asked them, "But who do you say I am?"

Simon Peter answered, "You are the Messiah, the Son of the living God."

*Jesus replied, "You are blessed, Simon son of John, because **my Father in heaven has revealed this to you.** You did not learn this from any human being. Now I say to you that you are Peter (which means 'rock'), and upon this rock I will build my church, and all the powers of hell will not conquer it."*[2]

Peter experienced a life-changing "aha" moment.

And, as Jesus was sitting with the tax collectors, He shared the parable of the lost son found in Luke, to help us learn of another "aha" moment.

"A man had two sons. The younger son told his father, 'I want my share of your estate now before you die.' So his father agreed to divide his wealth between his sons.

"A few days later this younger son packed all his belongings and moved to a distant land, and there he wasted all his money in wild living. About the time his money ran out, a great famine swept over the land, and he began to starve. He persuaded a local farmer to hire him, and the man sent him into his fields to feed the pigs. The young man became so hungry that even the pods he was feeding the pigs looked good to him. But no one gave him anything.

*"**When he finally came to his senses,** he said to himself, 'At home*

even the hired servants have food enough to spare, and here I am dying of hunger! I will go home to my father and say, "Father, I have sinned against both heaven and you, and I am no longer worthy of being called your son. Please take me on as a hired servant.'"[3]

Kyle Idleman describes these moments as "God-given moment[s] that change everything."[4] They are moments that open our eyes; moments revealed to us by God that finally bring us to our senses.

AND THEN THERE WAS KEVIN

As a kidmin leader, you have probably heard stories of kids in your ministry who struggle with learning from their "aha" moments. I remember Kevin coming to talk with me one stormy Sunday morning. He was a fifth grader at the time. Kevin's parents were known to be on the strict side. The storm outside was nothing in comparison to the storm raging within Kevin as he shared with me the rules and regulations mandated to be followed at home. He felt that he was never "good enough," because no matter how hard he tried he was told he could do better.

I ran into Kevin at a local grocery store a number of years later. Kevin was now nineteen years old, working in the produce department. As we began to catch up on life, I heard how he had run away from home to find a better life for himself. Kevin also shared how he hadn't set foot in any church in the past twelve years and had no intention of doing so in the future. When I asked him why, he said, "Well, I figure if my father's standards are so high at home, God's must be even higher. Nothing I will do will ever be good enough for either of them, so why bother?"

Before I could respond, Kevin was called to work in another area of the store. I wanted to follow him. I wanted to continue this conversation so Kevin could hear the truth about the God I knew, not the God he created to be his truth.

Kevin shared his "aha" moment that changed the spiritual direction of his life. Kevin's "aha" moment changed the spiritual direction of our ministry. Let me explain . . .

FIVE "AHA" MINISTRY MOMENTS

Well, I am taking a deep breath as I am writing this section because I know the pain of ministry "aha" moments, oh so well. As I embraced these "aha" moments, the light went on and revelation occurred. I can say when I truly accepted these lessons willingly and enthusiastically, true grit developed within me as a leader. I had some fun naming each moment for you. They aren't listed in any particular order. My prayer is for God to remind you of your "aha" moments as you read on.

#1 Which value wins?—This one explains how Kevin's story changed the spiritual direction of our ministry. Have you ever been in the place of making a leadership decision that didn't prove to be the best for your overall ministry purpose? I remember spending multiple hours every week with our volunteer teachers and programming teams to take a Bible story and creatively design how we were going to teach it within our different age groups. We knew no matter how creative we were in teaching the Bible story, *we needed to make sure the volunteer small group leaders had enough time in small group to be empowered to follow the Holy Spirit's promptings during discussion to truly help the kids apply the biblical truth to their everyday lives.* (By the way, we call this "relational discipleship.")

We tried to balance the amount of time given to leaders to be able to *relationally* build into the kids (to help them apply the story/truth to their week) with the amount of time given to large group teaching. After talking with Kevin, I found myself thinking about the balance of these two very important kidmin values. I decided to do a reality check and keep a weekly log of how much time both values were given each weekend in each room. You know what I found? Our time average was

70 percent large group and 30 percent small-group discussion! Now I could have listed multiple reasons why this time allocation happened. The creative elements took long in rehearsal, but we thought we could go faster in front of the kids. Or, the kids were so enjoying worship we felt it best if we extended worship time. What am I doing? All I am doing is making excuses for the imbalance.

How could any leader follow God's promptings when we were taking away time for them to guide the kids? How could a 30 percent small-group time change the views a child might have of God or His church by the relationship they had with their small group leader? Not much! Kevin's "aha" moment inspired me to make sure both values win. How do your ministry values show themselves each weekend? By looking at the time given to each value on the weekend, which one seems to always win out?

And Kevin? I haven't seen him again. I pray for him and I have placed his name on my desk so that I don't forget his story.

#2 Taking flight—Have you found yourself yearning to spread your wings a bit? I did, but staying the course felt safer and less chaotic. By staying quiet about this longing to spread my wings, it was very easy for church leadership to see me only as a well-placed "kid person" on staff. Not that there is anything wrong with being well placed, but I found myself feeling unsettled.

I ran across a quote by J. P. Morgan, the wealthy Gilded Age industrialist who was probably the most famous and admired man of his day. He observed, "The first step towards getting somewhere is to decide you're not going to stay where you are."

> **We can have the greatest impact when we lead with the question, "How can I help you win?"**

Where was I supposed to go? That question became the center of my prayer time with God. I began asking God to open doors for me to develop my leadership muscles—within or outside of our kids ministry. A month later the adventure began! I was asked to take a leadership role in a capital campaign at our church.. I found my emotions went from excitement to fear with shaking knees in a matter of minutes! But through this leadership experience I learned our God is faithful, powerful, never leaves me, and will never give up on me.

This opportunity was what God used to develop a different set of leadership muscles within me. It was the stepping-stone for church leadership to realize my heart wants the bigger picture of our church to win, not just our children's ministry. This opportunity gave me many "aha" moments about God, my team, and church leadership. One that has really stayed with me is that we kidmin leaders can have our greatest impact within the church structure when we lead with the question, "How can I help you win?"

#3 "That scares me!"—It was a chilly fall morning. My granddaughter and I went for a walk together. She couldn't help but notice the scary lawn ornaments displayed at that time of year. As we passed each one she kept saying, "That scares me." Have you ever been scared?

Eleanor Roosevelt grew up an awkward, timid child—but as First Lady she traveled widely and adventurously and became the eyes and ears of her husband, Franklin. She said, "Do one thing every day that scares you." Why would anyone want to do that? Well . . . doing something that scares you can stretch you to find out more about yourself, others, and God.

Our family was on a vacation where everyone wanted to try ziplining. Now being one who has a fear of heights, I kept telling everyone that would be great *for them*! Two days later I found myself in an orientation, learning how to use the equipment I was now wearing and getting ready to go hundreds of feet above ground. Why was I there?

Because I knew I would miss out on a bigger moment if I let my fear limit me.

To get to the top of the mountain, we needed to ride horses along a narrow path that had no guardrails! Once we got to the top we were told to remember to release our handgrip on the zipline. If we didn't, we would come to a full stop. Which wasn't a good move.

Our tour leader went first. Boy, did he make it look easy! Then our son, his wife, our daughter, and her husband went. It was now my turn. I remember fear taking over and my whole body beginning to shake. The tour guide made sure I was clipped to the zipline and then he told me it was time to let go.

I remember screaming the words "With my God I can scale a wall!" with my eyes closed. I began to feel the wind across my body, but my eyes were still closed. All of a sudden I was so afraid that instead of releasing my grip on the zipline, I squeezed so hard that I made a sudden stop two hundred feet in the air over a mountainous terrain. I couldn't move. I kept my eyes closed and continued to scream. Not a pretty sight (or sound)!

The tour guide ahead of me and the tour guide behind me raced to meet me in the middle. When they arrived they began to sing in such a soothing tone that I found myself opening my eyes to take a peek. Within minutes that felt like hours, they got me to release my grip, and I began to descend down the line. When I reached the platform I began to cry. Again, not a pretty sight!

We had fourteen more ziplines to go (!) until we were back where I could rip the equipment off and go home. Seven ziplines later, I found myself actually keeping my eyes open the whole time, enjoying the breathtaking views and praising God for His handiwork. As we continued, I became more relaxed and was able to really see the bigger picture.

Have you gripped fear more than gripping God to bring you and your ministry to a better place?

It was midmorning and I had five minutes before needing to meet with our senior pastor. I ran to his office, not wanting to be late. As he opened the door, I literally ran into him while breathing like I just finished running a marathon! Funny thing, but my breathing didn't settle down for a while. Here is a secret about me. I breathe fast when I find myself letting fear take over. I had to talk with him about a ministry strategy change that could make more work for people, bring about changes in structure, and require more money.

I explained that currently our ministry curriculum taught a different Bible story and big idea about God in every age level. No age group was ever on the same page. Even though we had purchased a new curriculum to implement, I felt it was time for a change. We needed to do the hard work, make necessary structure changes, and feel good about spending more funds that would allow us to teach the same Bible story in each age group every weekend so that parents could easily have faith conversations with their family. One story to discuss as a family instead of two to three! That would reap so many benefits.

Our senior pastor felt this new strategy seemed right, but then he asked, "What took you so long to come to this conclusion?" I was embarrassed to admit that moving in this direction literally scared me so that I lost focus of the bigger picture. Putting words to this fear was my first step toward the change that needed to follow.

"Ride it out, Pat. God will guide you. Don't let go of what you know to be best." Bill ended our conversation with those words. I was emboldened by his honesty. I wasn't scared. I was ready to take action!

#4 Wonder—Have you ever stopped seeing or expecting to see God's hand at work around you? Karen Mains, author of *The God Hunt*,[5] explains we must choose to recognize God anytime He intervenes in our everyday lives. Have you ever chosen fast pace over recognizing God while viewing your ministry with a sense of wonder or curiosity?

My (Matt's) "aha" moment came after working many hours and finding myself in a state of feeling overworked. Close friends and family tried to tell me to rest, but I couldn't find myself in a restful state, knowing all of the needs that needed to be met in leading a global, nonprofit children's ministry. My work environment didn't need to change. I did!

When I strive diligently to keep my ministry life and family life in balance, my wonder begins to rise. Instead of waiting on God, I expectantly know I will find Him. Wonder brings curiosity. Wonder brings creativity. Wonder brings an inner strength to make great decisions and to lead and inspire others.

#5 Enough!—Have you ever known a leader who loved change? Matt and I both do! Winston Churchill said, "There is nothing wrong with change, if it is in the right direction." You know what I learned? When I (Pat) constantly asked my team to switch direction just because I had an idea, I created what's called "change fatigue." There has to be a reason for the change, an explanation, a buy-in; but too many changes will spark confusion and frustration.

It was a leadership conference where John Maxwell was speaking. He challenged us with these words. "Learn to say 'no' to the good so you can say 'yes' to the best."

I left that session wondering if I was saying yes to the best or just creating change for change's sake. I decided to take two months and track the number of changes made within our ministry. I tracked the changes that affected our volunteers, our kids, and our parents.

I learned I was saying yes to everything, which didn't bring our very best work. I decided it was time to become a kidmin leader who created meaningful, lasting change. Even today I track the changes of my team and ministry. Discovering true ministry fruitfulness lies in learning the importance of "enough."

THE IMPACT OF "AHA"

Not all "aha" moments have equal ministry impact. Let me explain by sharing another "aha" ministry moment with you.

As a kidmin leader, I have wrestled for years with the best way to serve people with disabilities. When the families affected with disabilities enter our ministry doors, I can tell by looking into the parents' eyes how exhausted they feel. I have had many conversations with these families in which I learned the 24/7 intensity of doctor appointments, therapy, and school visits. Although some families are blessed with wonderful support, most are not. All share how they long for their time with God in our adult worship service.

For months, our volunteers and I have been praying about the best way to serve the whole family: parents, siblings, and the son or daughter with the disability. We had the right equipment donated to our ministry to help them engage. We had passionate volunteers with a special education background ready to serve. Still, something didn't seem right. We moved from one strategy to another in how to best serve them.

My "aha" moment came when I realized that even though it appeared the kids were being served, in reality they were only being served according to their *dis*ability, not their *ability*. These kids have amazing abilities! Rather than shaping their time in our ministry around what they could not do, we needed to make a change to create goals for each individual based on what they could do. Without these types of goals based on their abilities, we would be as typical as a school district. Were it not for this "aha" moment, I might have continued to try to remove them from a room when overstimulated instead of focusing on how to adapt the environment around their ability so that they could be integrated with the rest of the kids in our ministry.

After much prayer and review of the Scripture we already discussed in this chapter, I realized I needed to spend my time doing what matters most. In other words, I needed to answer the question: What steps should I take *after* the "aha" moment?

AFTER "AHA"

Pause and reflect. This was the first step I took once I believed in the "aha" moment that had come to me. I didn't just move forward. Remember, another change could have worsened the already existing "change fatigue" I referred to earlier. As stated at the beginning of the chapter, "aha" moments require prayer and discernment!

This step brings a kidmin leader to a place of moving from your gut intuition to observing, finding facts, and listening. It is a time to slow down. It is a time to follow what we learned from Adam and Eve: to open your eyes to the truth before you. It's a time to follow the Prodigal Son and recognize your current way of ministry. It's a time to ask some hard questions.

1. What will give this "aha" moment the most energy?
2. How will this "aha" moment bring the most success to your ministry's purpose?
3. What might your ministry need to do to create a win for the "aha" moment? In this case, I needed to think of our families, all the kids attending our ministry, our volunteers, and the bigger vision of our church.

HOW TO SOLICIT FEEDBACK

ALBERT EINSTEIN once said, "If you can't explain it simply, you don't understand it well enough." You need to be able to articulate your "aha" moment—and you need to solicit feedback. But how?

After you have your thoughts ready to explain in a simple manner, then it is time to get opinions from people you trust. Consider these questions to help you discern whom you want to ask.

1. Who is needed to join you in moving this "aha" moment forward?
2. What key parts of the church ministry might you consider in partnering with that will help this flash of insight move forward? How can you invite them to join you?
3. What key connections do you have with people who can help you enhance, extend, and leverage the "aha" moment?
4. Who are the top specialists in this particular area who should be joining you?

FOR ME (PAT), I KNEW I needed to include one person from student leadership with deep passion for this community because I would want this to be woven into the daily fabric of their ministry so the child would have the same experience as he/she got older; a staff member who brokers the campus rooms for weekend ministry use; and two special educators to give me and parents honest feedback.

This team helped me look and listen for any negativity. They provided accountability so I was able to stay focused and to move this "aha" moment toward reality.

It's on you. This last step is to remind you to take personal responsibility in moving this "aha" moment forward. Create an action plan that maps out the steps you need to take and their target dates. Refine your thoughts to be ready to share them simply with any person in your church's structure. Discern the best way to inspire your ministry to stay with this challenge.

Don't forget . . . every day is an opportunity to leverage your "aha" moments!

In closing, I pray you don't miss out on your bigger ministry moments. I pray you have the courage to slow down enough to have your eyes open. I know our heavenly Father will reveal them to you.

8

What Is Your Leadership Voice?

It's time we turn our attention to learning to demonstrate your unique voice—because when you find that true voice, you never know the impact you can have for Christ and His kingdom.

Several years ago I (Matt) was working for a Christian publisher in Nashville. We had an author who was madly in love with his suggested title for his book. Truth be told, it was an awful title! Not a single person in the marketing or publishing group liked it. It was cumbersome, long, it had an awkward flow to it, and we just didn't see it as a title that a customer would respond to. One day in the middle of all of this discussion, I requested a meeting with my boss to discuss the title. I shared with him a title that I thought was the perfect title based on the author's content, and my boss agreed—he actually loved my idea!

But there was one massive problem.

My boss said, "Matt, you are more than welcome to pitch your title to him if the opportunity presents itself, but you gotta understand, this author *loooves* his title. He just won't budge. We've tried."

Fast-forward to the day of the big meeting. The author was in town to discuss plans for his book with some of us. There were probably ten or twelve leaders in the room. The day got off to a great start, and the discussion was rolling along quite nicely. I really wanted to discern the best moment to lead the conversation to my suggested title, so I carefully watched how the discussion was navigating downstream.

My process of discerning, watching, and waiting paid off. At just the right moment, based on where the conversation had landed, I began to walk the author through my thinking. I delicately talked about the beauty of his message. Then I connected that to the need of the customer, and gently led the author to the realization of the cumbersome nature of his book title. I cautiously pointed out that many readers would not get to the beauty of his message because of the title. This led the author to ask me the question, "Do you have a better suggestion?" I responded by saying, "Well, that's your call, but I do have a suggestion that I think will resonate with readers and book buyers." And I shared it. The author went nuts! He loved it! When I got home that night I shared the good news with Katie, and we celebrated this moment over dinner.

Finding my leadership voice didn't just happen all at once—it took place in my preparation and by gaining permission from my senior leader ahead of time. But this front-end investment laid the groundwork for what became a big moment for me as a young leader. It was a time when I felt like I owned the room and really found my leadership voice from within.

Amy Jen Su and Muriel Maignan Wilkins, authors of the book (well) titled *Own the Room*, state no matter where you sit in an organization, you can "own the room" if you are able to do two things well: first, demonstrate your authentic value and distinction, and second, connect to others in a positive way.[1]

The first seven chapters of *Leading KidMin* focused on how to connect to others in a positive way. It's time we turn our attention to learning how to demonstrate your authentic voice and distinction. To better understand your voice of today, you need to go back and look at the seasons of your life.

A STRING OF SEASONS

Have you seen the movie *The King's Speech,* starring Colin Firth, Helena Bonham Carter, and Geoffrey Rush? It's an excellent film based on a true story, highlighting the different seasons found in one's life that can either help a person find or lose his or her voice. I highly recommend you watch it by yourself, but better yet, watch it with your team. The conversation following the movie can change the direction of your ministry!

When England's throne was suddenly thrust upon King George VI (Colin Firth) due to his brother's royal scandal, he knew he needed to lead the nation as a world war approached. King George had watched his father as king, so he knew the role extremely well. He loved his nation but there was one thing holding him back from being respected and followed—his voice. King George had to overcome a lifelong, debilitating speech impediment.

After his compassionate, determined wife, Elizabeth (Helena Bonham Carter), secretly found and hired an eccentric speech therapist (Geoffrey Rush), the two men forged a doctor/patient relationship that transformed into an unlikely friendship.

After their second appointment, the speech therapist knew he could help the king find his voice by training him on simple voice mechanics, but the impediment would never leave unless the therapist was able to better understand the root cause of why the stuttering began when the king was five years old. Without knowing the root cause, the stuttering would always limit the king's voice from being heard. The therapist knew there were seasons in the king's life that caused his stuttering.

As the king begins to be comfortable enough with the speech

therapist to reveal his life history, we learn of his string of seasons: seasons of his father never believing in him; seasons of being teased by his parents, siblings, and family members; seasons of wanting to express himself as a young boy by building model airplanes but his father forcing him to collect stamps as he had done; a season where he was beaten for being left-handed, and more.

I found myself crying as I watched and listened to the king describing season after season causing him to be governed by fear all of his life. The friendship and techniques learned by the king from his speech therapist ultimately empowered Britain's ruler to find his voice. The king was able to clarify and speak to what mattered most for his kingdom, which inspired his people and rallied the world during the dark days of World War II. The king turned from his fear to find his leadership voice. He brought a voice to what mattered most to him.

Moses had seasons in his life that led him to use his voice—or not. In Exodus 2, we read of Moses being put in a basket and raised by Pharaoh's daughter. In Exodus 2:11–17 we read about the season in Moses's life when he intervened after he saw an Egyptian mistreating an Israelite, killing the Egyptian man. Moses fled, to eventually find himself rescuing Jethro's daughters.

Exodus 3 to Exodus 14 continues to highlight Moses's seasons of life, beginning with God speaking to Moses through the burning bush. Moses, of course, found himself protesting, over and over, God's command to use his voice with Pharaoh. But he did—with Aaron's help—which led to the season of God's plagues upon Egypt, the Passover, and the triumphal crossing of the Red Sea.

Acts 7:22 reads, "Moses was taught all the wisdom of the Egyptians, and he was powerful in both speech and action." What moved Moses from fearful reluctance to use his voice against Pharaoh to becoming powerful in both speech and action? Like George VI in *The King's Speech*,

Moses turned from fear and found his leadership voice. Moses brought a voice to what mattered most to him.

SEEN AND NOT HEARD?

I (Pat) grew up in a home that believed and lived out the saying "a child should be seen and not heard." This notion meant I wasn't supposed to speak until I was spoken to, especially in the company of adults. My place was to be quiet, well-behaved, and do what I was told to do. Before both of my parents died, I was able to have conversations with them about why, as an adult, I believed my voice was not important. These conversations brought me to my root cause and understanding of their life.

Listening and understanding their childhood stories brought me to the realization they were only able to pass on what they possessed. My father spent most of his formative years in an orphanage, and my mother had an uninvolved father who enforced that same rule of silence whenever he walked through the door of her childhood home.

As I reflect over my life, I see God's hand at work as He brought multiple people and experiences to help me learn, believe, and use my voice in the different seasons of life. Teachers, colleagues, counselors, family, professional, and ministry opportunities—all played a part in helping me find my voice. Over a string of seasons, God used these encouragers and these experiences to bring me out of fear and give me the courage to use my voice in service of the calling He has placed in my life: that of raising spiritual champions.

Have you ever reflected over the seasons of your life that either gave you or took away your leadership voice? Can you clarify what matters most to you? Has your leadership voice been and does it continue to be heard by others? Is there anything in your life that might be diminishing your voice? What about the voices of your team? Who or what experiences has God brought into the seasons of your life that have brought your voice clarity?

REMEMBERING GOD'S TRUTH

There was a season of my life at Willow when I found myself enamored with the gifts and skills of other ministry leaders around me. "I wish I could cast a compelling vision like she does, God." "Why is it when I share an idea, no one seems to get it, but when John shared the same idea, everyone got on board?" These are some questions I wrote in my journal asking—or should I say complaining to—God about why my voice wasn't being heard. My desire to be heard drove me to be a leader who cared more about what others thought of me instead of remembering God's truth on how He sees and loves me. It wasn't until a friend spoke truth in what she saw me believing and acting upon that I faced up to my sin of idolizing others and giving them more power than what I was giving to God.

When we forget God's truth, we allow "towers" to build up in our heart and mind. These towers become the enemy of us finding the signature voice God purposely and lovingly gave us. Believing these towers over God's underlying truths really stifles and silences our voice.

> **"Why is it that when I share an idea, no one seems to get it, but when John shared the same idea, everyone got on board?"**

Take a look at the tower of Babel described in the book of Genesis. "At one time all the people of the world spoke the same language and used the same words. As the people migrated to the east, they found a plain in the land of Babylonia and settled there. They began saying to each other, 'Let's make bricks and harden them with fire.' (In this region bricks were used instead of stone, and tar was used for mortar.) Then they said, 'Come, let's build a great city for ourselves with a tower that reaches into the sky. This will make us famous and keep us from being scattered all over the world.'"[2]

The tower of Babel was a great human achievement, but it was a monument to the people wanting praise for themselves rather than God. What did God do? "The Lord scattered them all over the world, and they stopped building the city."[3]

What towers have you built in your life that silence your true voice and keep you captive? Finding your leadership voice from within means you are confident in God's truths and choose to put on the whole armor of God so that you don't allow any season of life to steal your voice. Finding your leadership voice within means you have razor-sharp clarity on God's purpose for your life. You are not timid to do your best in giving voice to this purpose, because you believe God placed it within you. Finding your leadership voice from within is the only way for you to be the best at what God called you to do.

This journey of self-discovery, to be the best you and speak your signature voice, will lead and influence the culture and the people of your church.

WHY PEOPLE DON'T SPEAK UP

A woman Matt and I both know was struck by the silence in her team meetings when she started a new job. "I came from a culture in my old job that was very freewheeling and opinionated," she says. "But I noticed when I joined the executive team in my new company that very few people weighed in at our periodic meetings. As the new person— and yes, as a woman—I was reluctant to speak up too much. But I kind of had to, in order to fill the vacuum. I noticed that the silence on the team was actually leading to bad decisions."

Marketing expert Kevin Daum wrote an article for Inc.com that unpacks the reasons "people sit back and say nothing when something really needs to be said."[4] Daum says, "So often people sit back and say nothing when something really needs to be said. It could be an idea, a suggestion, an observation, a criticism . . . but for some reason they don't want to speak up." The article is worth checking out online. One thing Daum notes that seems especially relevant to ministry contexts is the idea that people don't speak up because "the greater good should be the priority." We don't want to ruffle feathers, rock the boat, offend somebody.

But, says Daum, this is actually a selfish act—rather, we should speak up for the sake of the team's vision, which could open the eyes of others to see us as a powerful leader.

Becoming true kidmin change agents means we need to take seriously insights like these, and those shared by Amy Jen Su and Muriel Maignan Wilkins in the book titled *Own the Room*:

> Presence is what sets true leaders apart. It enables them to adapt to any situation and connect in a significant way with their stakeholders, all the while keeping sight of who they are as individuals. When we see our clients operate in that zone—where the substance of skills and the power of presence have come together —we know that they are operating at their best. They have *Signature Voice*: a unique leadership presence that is confident, authentic, and effective across a variety of situations and with diverse audiences. Like a signature, their presence is one that is recognizably unique and leaves a substantive impression on those around them and the organization. It takes this type of presence to own the room. . . . *your presence is unique to you.* You can find a presence that lets you be who you are and allows you to make an organizational impact in a way that is distinctly your own.[5]

IT'S TIME TO SPEAK UP!

The apostle Paul accomplished an astounding amount in two decades of ministry! Paul, imbued with the Holy Spirit and called by Jesus Christ, had, in effect, signature voice. He shares his belief, passion, and purpose in Philippians 3.

Paul's belief—"Yes, everything else is worthless when compared with the infinite value of knowing Christ Jesus my Lord. For his sake I have discarded everything else, counting it all as garbage, so that I could gain Christ and become one with him. I no longer count on my own righteousness through obeying the law; rather, I become righteous through faith in Christ. For God's way of making us right with himself depends on faith. I want to know Christ and experience the mighty power that raised him from the dead. I want to suffer with him, sharing in his death, so that one way or another I will experience the resurrection from the dead!"[6]

This Scripture explodes with Paul's passion for his calling. He knows what he stands for because he has identified his purpose and pursues it with grit, courage, and confidence.

Paul's purpose—"For I have told you often before, and I say it again with tears in my eyes, that there are many whose conduct shows they are really enemies of the cross of Christ. They are headed for destruction. Their god is their appetite, they brag about shameful things, and they think only about this life here on earth. But we are citizens of heaven, where the Lord Jesus Christ lives. And we are eagerly waiting for him to return as our Savior. He will take our weak mortal bodies and change them into glorious bodies like his own, using the same power with which he will bring everything under his control."[7]

Effective kidmin leaders are those who, like Paul, have figured out what they stand for, identified their purpose, and give voice to it with confidence, knowing they are giving their best to the glory of God. Like Paul, they face any towers, or any issues that are silencing their voice. They choose to stay away from a road to nowhere, allowing the unique purpose and passion given to them by God to shape all they do and influence all they lead. They fix their eyes on what is unseen, knowing God sees all.

YOUR KIDMIN LEADERSHIP VOICE REIMAGINED

Remember my (Matt's) story at the beginning of this chapter about the author and his book title? After all that strategic discussion with that author, we ended up not publishing the book. Sometimes, that's just how it goes. Well, years later, I was visiting another publisher in a different region of the United States. As I was waiting for my appointment to meet me in the lobby, I leaned against a bookshelf and my elbow nudged a book. I turned to look at the title on the spine, and there was my title staring me right in the face. I immediately scanned to see if it was the same author, and sure enough it was! That was a powerful moment for me personally.

Years ago, when I first encountered the author who had wonderful content but a not-so-wonderful title, I could have just kept my thoughts to myself. I gotta be honest, I'm so glad I didn't! What a blessing to see him soar, even if it was with a different publisher.

I believe that whole encounter in my life taught me something valuable: *when you find your authentic and unique leadership voice from within, you just never know the impact you can have* for *Christ and His kingdom.* Every day we are faced with a myriad of opportunities to lead, serve, speak up, influence, share, and act. As a kidmin leader, you hone your leadership voice from within. You build bridges to strategic partners within the local church. So that when your opportunity comes to speak, you are ready. Your time is now.

Pat and I pray you take the time to reimagine your signature voice for the sake of your kids ministry and your church. Find your true voice. It will pave the way to inspire and motivate others to join you in changing the game. Your signature voice will give you the strength needed for optimism, grit, confidence, and creativity . . . what every kidmin change agent needs!

9

You: Winning!

Every kidmin leader will face battles . . . but we have to "charge the hill" with love, purpose, and grit as we strive for the vision God has placed in our hearts.

My husband and I decided to take a train trip to visit a few national parks: Glacier, Grand Teton, and Yellowstone, to name a few. The national parks were spectacular as we traveled in awe of the vibrant fall colors, waterfalls, bears, and bison. As we were nearing one of the parks, we decided to visit an Indian reservation that put on a reenactment of the pioneers' move westward and their encounters with Native Americans. As we watched the true-life drama unfold, we heard a shotgun go off. All of a sudden, right before our eyes, we were in the midst of a battlefield!

Have you ever seen a battle in a movie? Battles are ignited when two opposing viewpoints collide and any peaceful resolution is ruled out. One side, trying to gain victory, decides to charge up the battle hill with full force (or stage a surprise attack, or outflank the enemy, or . . . you get the idea!). The other side valiantly tries to hold its ground and return fire. Eventually, hours or days later, one side surrenders. As the battle smoke clears, those left can see the human toll taken by the conflict.

Ministry battles may be less bloody, but they exact a human toll of another sort. When these battles grind on, wounds turn into scars. I have seen the life taken out of someone's dream because he chose to stuff his true emotions and allowed another ministry to charge the hill and take control. The outward battle may have ended . . . but the inward conflict was still raging.

I believe every kidmin leader will face ministry and personal battles, especially when God is calling you to change the game. Our posture must be to charge the hill with love, purpose, and grit as we strive for the vision God has placed in our hearts.

WHAT IS THE PRICE OF WINNING?

Twenty-eight years of ministry has opened my eyes to the journey a kidmin leader experiences as she or he stays the course when conflict is brewing. During my ministry, I've often been reminded of the famous saying, "Don't win the battle and lose the war."

This warning has served my ministry well. When I am more focused on the short-term results to the neglect of the long-term, I am only winning the battle, not the war. I remember a time when I was faced with such a decision . . .

Church leadership was about to challenge our congregation to show their solidarity with those who were struggling across the world. The strategy was set. The dates were chosen. The experience was about to be launched. As I looked at the plans for this vision, I had a choice to make. Do I stand firm and push the way *I* felt our kids and families should participate in this church-wide compassion strategy, or do I listen, ask questions, and shape what was already planned by church leadership so our families could fully participate?

I chose the latter. Why? As I dug into what was really bothering me, I realized it wasn't because church leadership didn't have a good plan in place. It was because I hadn't been a voice around the planning table. (Can you relate?) My frustration was my problem, not theirs. Allowing my frustration to fuel my decision to power up on them to "win" the dispute could have lost our ministry the chance to have church leadership as a ministry partner moving forward. When we focus on the battle and charge up the hill because we believe we have the right to "win," a bitter aftertaste in the lives of everyone involved is the outcome. When you find yourself in a ministry battle, ask yourself this question: am I prepared to pay the price for the pleasure of winning the battle?

THE FIGHT AGAINST FEAR

We as kidmin leaders can fight battles that rage within us, unseen by others. We fight fear as it whispers in our ear: *"Don't say anything."* We don't want to look stupid. We sit mute in meetings when we should speak up. We put off having a crucial conversation.

It happened to me . . .

I was engaged in a meeting discussing the reasons more people weren't joining the recovery groups that met at our church on Monday nights. We believed people shied away because Monday nights began to be seen as the night when "those people with serious problems" met. As I was sitting in the meeting, God brought an idea of transitioning our Monday night groups to join Wednesday nights, which

THINGS WE THINK WHEN WE'RE AFRAID

- *I might fail.*
- *I doubt I can do it.*
- *I will have to work too hard.*
- *I will be outside my comfort zone.*
- *I can't disappoint my senior pastor.*
- *I don't know how to start.*
- *What will people think?*

was already known to be our discipleship night, filled with classes and teaching. I remember pushing these thoughts down as our conversations continued, not wanting to speak up at all. Before I knew it, I said every one of the "justifying fear" statements in my mind to justify why I needed to keep my mouth shut. Even though I knew God wanted me to be the one to run point on this new plan, I decided it was time to zip my lips!

Have you ever been in a team conversation where you had a moment of clarity that frightened you so much that you chose to believe your fear more than you believed God was calling you to be a change agent? As I tried to sit on the idea instead of sharing it in our meeting, I found the suppressed war raging inside of me. I was facing a decision. Do I choose fear to win or do I choose to trust God and let His plan win? It felt as if this internal war went on for hours, but in reality, it didn't last more than twenty seconds.

I swallowed hard, asking God to keep me quiet if what I was about to say wasn't from Him. All of a sudden an inner confidence began to crush my fear as I found myself speaking up and sharing God's idea. I had a peace that only God could have given me. If I would have allowed my fear to take me hostage, only God knows how long it would have taken our congregation to become a community that supports people in their efforts to dig deep to understand their life challenges.

Do you know when fear is in charge of your kidmin decisions about when or how to change the game? Consider tracing back to the origin of each fear. I have found when I acknowledge my fear and study where it came from, I can make better intentional choices to keep it from controlling my decisions, and I move from being a survivor toward what I would like to call a hero.

Kidmin heroes find themselves anticipating their battles and fight them on their knees. Before the battle begins, at the core of who they are, they do whatever it takes to create a collaborative culture, persuading others to join them, praying all the way.

Jesus anticipated His battle before He found himself arrested and in front of Pontius Pilate. Jesus conquered in the battle with Pilate's judgment because He prayed the night before, anticipating the battle and gaining victory before His struggle began. "Then Jesus went with them to the olive grove called Gethsemane, and he said, 'Sit here while I go over there to pray.' He took Peter and Zebedee's two sons, James and John, and he became anguished and distressed. He told them, 'My soul is crushed with grief to the point of death. Stay here and keep watch with me.' "[1]

Knowing harm would come his way, Daniel overcame the wrath of King Darius because he prayed. Even though Daniel knew King Darius signed the law that allowed prayer only to the king, Daniel was about to enter a battle with the king by being put into the lion's den. Daniel entered the battle with strength.[2]

And Peter had a miraculous escape from prison because "while Peter was in prison, the church prayed very earnestly for him."[3]

Friends, prayer changes the battlefield. Prayer turns the kidmin survivor into a kidmin hero who leads confidently, believing God will prevail! The kidmin hero doesn't make demands, attack, or seek to control. The kidmin hero doesn't overreact, and can shift his or her thinking in a rational direction; not allowing negative thoughts to flood their mind, focusing energy on what matters most. The kidmin hero excels at taking stock of the facts at hand to move a culture bruised by battles to a culture of health and collaboration.

STEVE JOBS AND DENZEL WASHINGTON

I (Matt) am a huge football fan: college football, NFL, football movies, you name it. I particularly love the Disney movie *Remember the Titans*. Both Pat and I can watch this movie—which is based on the true story of a team in Civil Rights–era Virginia—over and over again! Denzel Washington plays a hotheaded coach who realizes he needs to collaborate, not battle, with his other football coaches if he wants to turn a disorganized football team into a racially mixed, disciplined outfit.

I was surprised as I read an article about Steve Jobs asking his successor, Tim Cook, to watch *Remember the Titans* with him a few days before his death.[4] According to the article, Jobs had little interest in sports. Jobs choosing to watch this type of movie really surprised Cook: "Why would Jobs, who had recently stepped down as Apple CEO and appointed Cook in his place, want to watch this movie with his successor just a few days before he died? Was he trying to pass on some crucial knowledge?"[5]

Writer Leander Kahney speculates on what Jobs might have been trying to do: "Overall, the movie is about teamwork and leadership. It's about creating a disciplined organization. It's about studying the plays, making plans and executing. It's about forcing individuals to overcome their prejudices and hostility to work as a team. Through leadership, the Bad News Bears are transformed into the Undefeated Titans."[6]

> **Silos pop up in all kinds of churches and ministries, no matter how big or how small.**

With leading a new way, ministry is transformed. Without the heart of focusing on long-term results, leading with confidence and fighting with prayer, ministry battles surface. When ministry battles surface, most try to charge the hill because their motive is to put a stake into the ground. As we discussed in detail in chapter 6, we learned that just over 88 percent of those kidmin leaders we surveyed really feel the need to collaborate and strategize with other ministries. And just over 65 percent of those surveyed don't feel their church *can* actually collaborate, strategize, and lead across the different ministry areas. That disparity can lead to conflicts between the different ministry areas, stuck in their silos. And trust us: silos pop up in all kinds of churches and ministries, no matter how big or how small!

NO MORE SILOS!

Patrick Lencioni, author of *Silos, Politics and Turf Wars,*[7] tackles the frustration many organizations have by teammates working in silos. Lencioni's book describes silos as the invisible barriers that "separate work teams, departments and divisions, causing people who are supposed to be on the same team to work against one another."[8] According to Lencioni, the silos and turf wars waste resources, derail organizations, and jeopardize results.

I (Pat) have seen that happen, and I have been instrumental in making that happen for our church. For many years, our kidmin and student ministries worked in silos. If you asked us, we would have probably said we sensed a need to move from working in silos to collaborating, but the reality was we worked in silos! Silos were easier, less complicated, and didn't take relational energy; however, silos served the directors more than the kids and families we were here to serve.

We (children and youth directors) decided to design an intentional curriculum that went from birth through high school. Now to some of you, this might sound like a simple task. Not to us! We knew this audacious goal would only be accomplished if we took the hours needed to better understand the teaching content, philosophy, and program of each ministry. We needed to come in ready to seek to understand, not with a judgmental attitude.

What we thought would take us two days to complete actually took us months. We had the passion but we found our perseverance beginning to ebb. Neither of us consciously decided to disengage, but that was the outcome, which led us to wanting to work in our silos and protect our turf. As I look back to that time frame of ministry, I now understand why we faced that outcome.

When we first began our work together, we did so out of compliance. We complied with the need to do something, but we were avoiding working together. It wasn't until an objective outside leader named Heather was asked to lead us as a group that we finally started to consider there might be a better way to accomplish this goal. We were all protecting our ministry "turf." We had some joint discussions before this outside leader became the point person of this team, but my focus was still on my ministry's individual curriculum decisions rather than on what a collective strategy might look like. Heather brought us to a place of tasting the sweetness of collaboration. What was the outcome of this collaboration? Unity! As a unified team we developed a joint curriculum that leveraged our combined resources, ideas, and talents. With Heather's persuasion, influence, and accountability, we truly became collaborative, putting our best energy toward changing the game of our Next Gen curriculum.

Together, we paused to look at ministry gaps from one ministry to another. We looked at why each ministry exists, to make sure it met a need of our kids and students. We prayed together for God to guide us as one collective union. We planned the best pathway of sharing this new curriculum design with all our volunteers together. We didn't leave a meeting without deciding next steps and what team members needed to work together to bring us to a place of designing next best steps that would help our ministries align with this grander vision. We kept each other accountable. We kept short accounts so that relationships would remain strong.

What's interesting is we didn't consciously decide not to collaborate. At that time, collaboration was not a part of our church's culture. Instead, we did what came naturally to each of us, which was to work on our own. This experience showed me true collaboration is time-consuming. It requires me to be good with losing the battle to win the war; engaging with confidence, not fear; praying all the way. It requires *patient persistence.*

ABIGAIL CHANGES THE GAME

Proverbs 25:15 reads, "Patience can persuade a prince, and soft speech can break bones." True collaboration is hard for me at times because I want to challenge and state what I believe is right. God has shown me that for me to change the game, my posture needs to follow Proverbs 25:15 and I need to engage in give-and-take discussions with a gentle heart and gentle speech. With it, I am persuading others to collaborate so collectively we can achieve outstanding results.

Persuasive speech is what saved Nabal in 1 Samuel 25. Nabal's wife Abigail was more suited than her husband to manage his wealth. In spite of Nabal's shortcomings, his household did what they could to keep him out of trouble. Many commentaries note that this loyalty was probably inspired by Abigail.

First Samuel 25:7–8 explains the reason behind the request David made of Nabal. "While your shepherds stayed among us near Carmel, we never harmed them, and nothing was ever stolen from them. Ask your own men, and they will tell you [Nabal] this is true. So would you be kind to us, since we have come at a time of celebration? Please share any provisions you might have on hand with us and with your friend David."

Simple hospitality demanded that travelers, any number of them, be fed. David and his men had been protecting Nabal's workforce, and part of Nabal's prosperity was due to David's vigilance at protecting him. But Nabal rudely refused David's request to feed his six hundred men, even though he was very rich and could have easily afforded to do so. Once David's men returned to David to tell him what Nabal had said, David was furious.

"'Get your swords!' was David's reply as he strapped on his own . . . Meanwhile, one of Nabal's servants went to Abigail and told her, 'David sent messengers from the wilderness to greet our master, but he screamed insults at them. These men have been very good to us, and we never suffered any harm from them . . . You need to know this and figure out what to do, for there is going to be trouble for our master and his whole family.' . . . When Abigail saw David, she quickly got off her donkey and bowed low before him. She fell at his feet and said, 'I accept all blame in this matter, my lord. Please listen to what I have to say. I know Nabal is a wicked and ill-tempered man; please don't pay any attention to him. He is a fool, just as his name suggests. But I never even saw the young men you sent . . . Please forgive me if I have offended you in any way.' "[9]

By Abigail's swift actions and skillful negotiation, she kept David from taking vengeance upon Nabal.

"David replied to Abigail, 'Praise the Lord, the God of Israel, who has sent you to meet me today! Thank God for your good sense! Bless you for keeping me from [murdering Nabal] and from carrying out vengeance with my own hands.' "[10]

Abigail saw the big picture and used her skills to promote peace. She played a significant role in changing the course with David. She lived out Proverbs 25:15 while Nabal lived out Proverbs 15:1, which reads, "A gentle answer deflects anger, but harsh words make tempers flare." Abigail changed the game without charging up the hill. Nabal's bad attitude almost touched off a battle.

A NEW WAY

Friends, God *is* calling you to find a new way. You can be the first one to change the culture direction of your church (or join others who have gone ahead of you) to overcome fear, relational issues, the desire to protect your turf. Choose the new way. Fight your battles on your knees. When you choose a new way, then, and only then, will you win—for the sake of the Kingdom.

The Journey Forward

When Katie and I were first married, we were invited to serve as small group leaders for twelve first-graders. Of all of our shared experiences in life, it's difficult to think of one that was more transforming than this one.

God used this experience to open up our eyes to what the Holy Spirit can do in the life of a child when their heart is open to His Word. During this part of our journey we experienced leading kids to Christ, watching their eyes open up to the wonder of God, seeing kids engaged in local ministry service, and watching gospel fruit in the lives of kids. This experience truly changed Katie and me because we saw firsthand that children's ministry is a very fruitful place of ministry. We wanted more. We asked for more. God gave us that opportunity.

Our children's pastor at the time, Jeff, worked with Katie and me to become the volunteer elementary ministry directors. As volunteers, we oversaw a ministry of about eighty kids in small groups each week. As a young married couple, we were responsible for equipping volunteers, staffing volunteers, providing an environment of inspiration, and striving for increased ministry effectiveness for the sake of leading kids to know, love, and serve the Lord Jesus Christ.

Not long after serving in this ministry role, we began to notice areas of kids ministry that needed improvement, needed fixing, needed redesigning . . . needed change. It was during this experience nearly twenty years ago that God, for the first time, allowed Katie and me to begin cutting our teeth on leading change within children's ministry. And to be honest, in one form or another, it hasn't stopped.

Each and every one of us comes from a different context. For me, it was starting out in a volunteer position leading a ministry of eighty kids and approximately twelve leaders—and now serving within a global children's ministry. For Pat, it was working in one of the most well-known megachurches in North America. And you have your own unique story and set of circumstances. But no matter who you are, or where you are, there is one constant in kids ministry.

Our country's culture is facing change at a rapid pace. So is the church. But what can match this rate of change? As we stand on the mountaintop and look back at the trek through this book, we propose that *you,* as the kidmin leader, are the catalyst needed to face change head-on. But what do we mean by this? Are we proposing that you be some sort of superhero who will swoop in at the last second and make it all right? Certainly not! But you *are* a game changer . . . you *are* a catalyst who can lead and influence your local church to a place of more effective children's ministry.

But how?

As you journey forward in your trek, remember that we can't completely rely on the out-of-the-box trend-solution to be our answer. Trends exist to inform us, but not to own us. You are the kind of leader that asks, "What can we learn from this trend? And how does this trend-solution influence and assimilate into my local context?" You also realize that in order to be understood clearly, you must gain perspective on how others view you in order to receive the warmer affection known as "favor" from your senior leaders. And this will require that you listen honestly, even when at times, you just want to run away. Because you deeply desire to be most effective in ministry, you realize you can't lead authentic change without inviting others into your ministry to speak honest words to shape your ministry to be more effective.

By the power and strength of our Lord and Savior Jesus Christ, you can do this.

You also realize that what you are doing in children's ministry is not an appendage to the local church. Rather, what you do in helping kids come to know, love, and serve Jesus is central to the mission of the church. Because of this, alignment to the overall mission, vision, values, and culture is critical to you. One of the ways to achieve this high level of alignment you are aiming for is simply knowing the heartbeat of your senior pastor, and gaining his favor. You will work diligently to establish an increasingly healthy relationship with your lead pastor(s) and will work within the time constraints given to invest heavily in this relationship, clothing yourself in a posture of gratitude and stewardship for the time you are given. You will be relentless. You will not give up in being a student of your senior leaders, and they will notice your humble posture and the grit you possess in building a strong partnership with them. They will sense that you are "for" them and a strong, active partner in the ministry. The way you build partnerships and alliances with the right leaders, parents, and volunteers within your local ministry will become the fruit that you are truly building a win-win-win: A win for your partners and their ministry areas; a win in the lives of the kids, students, and families you serve; and a win for the ministry effectiveness of your kidmin.

By the power and strength of our Lord and Savior Jesus Christ, you can do this.

Your dependency upon the Holy Spirit—His power, His strength, His wisdom, and His passion to see kids and parents come to know, love, and follow Him—this deep dependency will be the secret of your ministry. You will lean into Him, listening intently for His voice and direction. You will be on the lookout for those "aha" moments," capturing them, and praying over them to discern His direction in your local kids ministry. At this point in your journey you know that you have a certain set of responsibilities, dreams, and plans that will help kids come closer to Jesus and follow Him in lifelong discipleship.

Like Moses, you have a calling and you realize that God is asking you to be the voice to speak on behalf of reaching kids and families. That's a big responsibility! You realize just how big a responsibility this is, and you are committed to honing your voice as you are given opportunities to speak up. The stewardship of these opportunities is taken so seriously that you will be relentless in finding your kidmin leadership voice that connects to the hearts, minds, and ears of your listeners. In your white-hot passion to reach kids and make disciples, you will be tempted to charge the hill. You may even be tempted to trample over something or someone to see your ministry vision come to life. But your uncommon dependency upon the Holy Spirit will remind you that the pathway forward is about leading differently, not trampling over others on your way to top of the hill of fruitful ministry. Your leadership can be a game changer.

By the power and strength of our Lord and Savior Jesus Christ, you can do this.

Psalm 121 says,

> I look up to the mountains—
>   does my help come from there?
> My help comes from the Lord,
>   who made heaven and earth!

He will not let you stumble;
> the one who watches over you will not slumber.

Indeed, he who watches over Israel
> never slumbers or sleeps.

The Lord himself watches over you!
> The Lord stands beside you as your protective shade.

The sun will not harm you by day,
> nor the moon at night.

The Lord keeps you from all harm
> and watches over your life.

The Lord keeps watch over you as you come and go,
> both now and forever.

These words found in the book of Psalms soothed my soul and helped me see God's thumbprints as He developed my (Pat's) new posture of leadership, especially on those dark, lonely days when I felt we were just standing still.

Recently I discovered these words by Hillsong pastor Brian Houston: "Living in the faith lane isn't a paint-by-numbers picture. It colors outside the lines and sees with different eyes than the world does— eternal eyes with eternal perspective. Your heavenly Father didn't create you to live a life of mediocrity. He created you to live a life in the faith lane."[1]

Living in the faith lane in kids ministry has many turns and detours, and at times you can find yourself facing one mountain after another because you are trying to get to the "final" destination. We all have a final destination of what we want our kid ministries to be known for. All that is good, but our ministry really isn't about the final destination. It's about becoming a new you and seeing every situation before you through eternal eyes. It's about inviting God to do His transforming work. Our kidmin change-agent faith lanes are held in the arms of a loving God who always pursues our best interest. When we trust God, knowing He has the perfect plan and the perfect timing, and allow Him to open our eyes, a new posture of leadership will be developing within us.

Kidmin change agents (that's you!), let's refocus our energies and be open to a new way of leading as we remain humble and open, having the perseverance and grit to approach those on the kidmin journey with us with love, purpose, and influence.

Will adversity come our way? Absolutely! It's all part of the faith-lane journey. Consider committing to nurture and reinvest in the practices and processes this book has brought you and your team. The best kidmin change agents are constantly evaluating their vision, through listening to others, identifying gaps, aligning with the grander vision and then acting on the opportunities before them. With God's leadership in your life, you have what it takes to lead with grit and be a change agent in your church. You never have to be afraid or discouraged on your journey. His love will never fail you. Let Him satisfy your soul. Be confident. Follow Him forward. You are leading kidmin, which is His unique purpose and plan for you to "become," so that His kingdom can be brought to this broken world. He chose you to be His kidmin change agent. God is your primary encourager, and we are cheering you on!

Pat Cimo
Matt Markins

Notes

Chapter 2: Gaining Clarity: For Yourself, For Others

1. Michael Myatt, "Culture: Don't Copy – Create," Forbes.com, June 27, 2012, http://www.forbes.com/sites/mikemyatt/2012/06/27/ culture-dont-copy-create/#25606e9229a1.

Chapter 4: Aligning to a Larger Vision

1. Whitney Stewart, *Who Was Walt Disney?* (New York: Grosset & Dunlap, 2009), 91–93.
2. Bill Scollon, *Walt Disney: Drawn from Imagination* (New York: Disney Press, 2014), 98, 103, 100.
3. Martin Gitlin, *Walt Disney: Entertainment Visionary* (Minneapolis: ABDO Publishing, 2010), 67–68.
4. Patrick Lencioni, *The Advantage* (San Francisco: Jossey-Bass), 2012.
5. Jim Collins, "Aligning Action and Values," *The Forum*, June 2000.
6. Luke 1:13, 16.
7. Collins, "Aligning Vision and Values."

Chapter 5: How to Be a Student of Your Senior Pastor

1. Craig Groeschel, *It* (Grand Rapids: Zondervan, 2008).
2. Philippians 2:1–4.

Chapter 6: Building Partnerships That Work

1. Mark 11:23b–25.
2. Hebrews 12:1–2.
3. Hebrews 12:11.
4. Hebrews 12:15.

Chapter 7: Listening to Those "Aha" Moments

1. Kyle Idleman, *Aha* (Colorado Springs: David C. Cook, 2014).
2. Matthew 16:13–18, emphasis added.
3. Luke 15:11–19, emphasis added.
4. Idleman, *Aha*, 19.
5. Karen Mains, *The God Hunt* (Downers Grove, IL: InterVarsity, 2003).

Chapter 8: What Is Your Leadership Voice?

1. Amy Jen Su and Muriel Maignan Wilkins, *Own the Room* (Cambridge, MA: Harvard Business School Publishing, 2013).
2. Genesis 11:1–4.
3. Genesis 11:8.
4. Kevin Daum, "5 Reasons You Should Speak Up (Even When You Think You Shouldn't)," Inc.com, February 28, 2014, http://www.inc.com/kevin-daum/5-reasons-you-should-speak-up-even-when-you-think-you-shouldnt.html.
5. Su and Wilkins, *Own the Room*, 2, 5.
6. Philippians 3:8–11.
7. Philippians 3:18–21.

Chapter 9: You: Winning!

1. Matthew 26:36–38.
2. Daniel 6:1–28.
3. Acts 12:5.
4. Leander Kahney, "Why Did Steve Jobs Make Tim Cook Watch Remember the Titans?", cultofmac.com, March 19, 2015, http://www.cultofmac.com/316220/why-did-steve-jobs-make-tim-cook-watch-remember-the-titans/.
5. Ibid.
6. Ibid.
7. Patrick Lencioni, *Silos, Politics and Turf Wars* (San Francisco: Jossey Bass, 2006).
8. *Silos, Politics and Turf Wars*, The Table Group, http://www.tablegroup.com/books/silos.
9. 1 Samuel 25:13a, 14–15a, 17a, 23–25, 28a.
10. 1 Samuel 25:32–33.

The Journey Forward

1. Brian Houston, *Live Love Lead* (New York: FaithWords, 2015), 13.

A Word about the Research

P at and I (Matt) would like to take a moment to thank three essential partners who helped us conduct the research contained in *Leading KidMin*.

THE SURVEY

We partnered with Mark McPeak of Sightline Research, based out of Nashville, to build the survey. Mark has been conducting qualitative and quantitative research projects since 1989 with organizations and companies like the Ford Motor Company, Harper Collins Christian Publishing, Caterpillar Financial, The Gideons International, the Tennessee Titans, Hunt Brothers Pizza, Trevecca Nazarene University, Awana, and a long list of local churches.

http://sightlineresearch.com/

THE 340 RESPONDENTS

In order to reach kidmin leaders like you (the 340 leaders who filled out the survey), we partnered with our friends from the D6 Conference and Children's Pastors' Conference. These two leading conferences, both of which attract kidmin leaders, shared the survey with their audiences. Gathering the needed responses would not have been possible without the help and support of these two ministries.

D6 is a ministry of Randall House Publishers based out of Nashville. Randall House is a Christian publisher and home of D6 Family Ministries, dedicated to promoting the cause of Christ, generational discipleship, and serving both the church and home through curriculum, books, and events. CPC (Children's Pastors' Conference) is a ministry of INCM (International Network of Children's Ministries) based out of Elgin, Illinois. The mission of INCM is to be a connecting platform for training, resourcing, and inspiring those who minister to children and their families. Thank you once again for the trust and for your tremendous support.

http://d6family.com/d6-conference/

http://www.childrenspastorsconference.com/

NOW IT'S YOUR TURN: DISCUSSION GUIDE

AFTER WE READ a book and discover helpful insights, many of us can put those insights into practice by talking about our discoveries with others. Here's a short discussion guide you can use on your own or with your team.

KNOWING AND SHARING YOUR VISION

Challenge A: In your personal reflection and/or with your team, ask yourself the following questions about your dream for your mission.

1. What is the purpose of your kids ministry?
2. Is your purpose clear to each person who engages in your ministry? (Leadership above you? Those you lead? Volunteers? Parents? Children?)
3. What results do you see in your kids ministry that show your ministry is on the right track toward your mission?
4. Describe some small victories your kids ministry had over the past year moving toward your mission?
5. How is God moving in your church? And, how would your dream extend the mission of your church? (If it will not extend the mission of your church, be careful . . . this could be an indication that your dream is more about you, and less about God's mission for your church.)
6. Do you know the best way to communicate your ministry to each person who engages in your ministry?

Once you answer these questions, try putting the answers in a one-page summary sheet to keep in front of your team.

If you've ever mowed your lawn (and many of us have cut a lot of grass in our day!), the best way to know how straight your lines are is to stop and look at your previous rows and assess alignment. The answers to the questions above will help you begin to see if your children's ministry purpose and your dream for the future are in alignment, which will help bring about the needed clarity. It's important that you take the time to think through this. If you don't see the alignment and have clarity, others will certainly not be able to have clarity around your children's ministry purpose, mission, and values and how they align with the larger direction of your church.

Challenge B: In your personal reflection and/or with your team, ask yourself the following questions to help you discover any limits to your ministry finding favor with church leadership.

1. Think of your church ministry culture. Would you define it as an environment where different ministries want to come together?
2. Think of church strategies implemented over the past six months. As you look at how these strategies moved forward, were they silo driven with one way of accomplishing the purpose or were they collaboratively driven to bring many ways to work on the common purpose? List the reasons you chose your answer.
3. Think of your church vision and mission scale. Choose which best describes your church's vision and mission:

    a. Significantly underdeveloped   b. Underdeveloped

    c. In development   d. Developed

    e. Well developed

4. Think of your relationship with your senior pastor. Are there any relational obstacles that might be limiting you and your senior pastor's desire for your church and your ministry being more aligned?
5. Think of your relationship with other church leadership. Would you describe these relationships as solid, trusting relationships? Why or why not?

After reviewing your answers to the above questions, is the favor your ministry is experiencing from church leadership heading in a positive direction? Consider putting together a list of action items you or your ministry must do to increase favor toward you. Take your list to God on a daily basis. He has a message to tell you!

Challenge C: Once you are able to temporarily "pop your head up" and rise above the urgent week-to-week demands, ask yourself (or your team) the following questions to help you discern your ministry perspective.

1. Is your ministry pace limiting you from having a clear perspective on how others see your ministry? Why or why not?
2. What big ministry wins have you experienced over the last six months?
3. Reviewing your list from question 2, why did you consider each to be a big win for your ministry?

4. What best practices are you pursuing that easily align with your kidmin dream/purpose?

5. What best practices are you pursuing that easily align with your church's culture?

GETTING IN SYNC WITH YOUR CHURCH

Working through ministry alignment is absolutely critical. Working through these questions will help your team understand the importance of being in sync with the greater vision of your church.

Are you aligned with the greater vision of your church or are you competing with the greater vision of your church?

How would others assess the children's ministry in your church?

Is your kids ministry remaining true to your church's timely core values, or are your kidmin policies and practices becoming *most* important to you and your team? Who needs to take action in fixing this?

BUILDING PARTNERSHIPS THAT WORK

Think of your ministry. What dream has God been placing on your heart that He wants you to move forward? What other ministry partnerships do you need to build so that this dream becomes a reality? As you discern who to partner with, how will this partnership help you focus on what your ministry does best yet bring a larger impact? Do you have a dream in mind?

Now, write it down and include the date. Ask God to guide you. Ask Him to show you what concrete actions you now need to take to grow healthy partnerships that will affect change and make this dream a reality. Then, once a month, go back to the dream and date you wrote. I know you will be reminded of God working through you because you will find this dream becoming your reality.

Acknowledgments

I (Pat) remember the day and place where I felt God telling me this book is part of His plan for me. God, You gave me the courage to follow through in making *Leading KidMin* a reality. Your love and faithfulness never left me. You never gave up on me when the blank page I held before You made my hand quiver. You reminded me of your grace and power. You brought Your comfort through others, whom I want to humbly thank.

I want to thank my husband, Dave, for standing beside me throughout writing this book. You have been my inspiration, motivation, rock, and safe place. I love you forever.

I also thank my wonderful children, Michelle, Dennis, Scott, and Ashley, along with our grandchildren, Jenna, Taryn, Dave, and Ellie. On those days I needed to stay focused on writing this book instead of us being together, you always understood why. Your hugs, smiles, and encouragement told me you would always be on my side. Each of you blesses my life and I love being your mom, Nonni, and friend.

To Willow staff and volunteers, I thank you for sharing ministry with me. Many of you shared your happiness and encouragement when it seemed too difficult to complete. I especially want to thank Lara-Lyn, Kirsten, Paul, Debbie, Nancy, Shalise, Cary, Mindy, and Amy.

Bill Hybels and Willow's leadership team, thank you for casting vision and creating multiple opportunities for women to be in leadership.

Willow has been the community where I have become and continue to grow as a change agent leader. Without you, your challenge, and openness, I wouldn't be able to write my *Leading KidMin* journey. I will be forever grateful.

Finally, I thank my extended family. Your constant support and encouragement gave me strength to stay the course. Each of you fills my heart. I am so grateful for you.

To my friend and coauthor, Matt: I thank you for devoting your knowledge, passion, skills, and effort to "our" vision that over time became *Leading KidMin*. You have an amazing commitment to collaboration.

I (Matt) would like to first thank God my Father for the ongoing and daily opportunity I'm given to be Your son and disciple. You are a good Father. Most of the ministry opportunities I've been given by You fall into the "leading change" space, and I'm thankful for the Holy Spirit's ongoing sharpening in the crucible of the disciple's journey.

Katie, your deep spiritual wisdom is only surpassed by your pursuit of the Giver of wisdom. As your husband, I reap the daily fruit of your friendship and companionship. More days together with you is my satisfying earthly reward: I see Christ in you each and every day. Warren and Hudson, you guys are always challenging me to think critically in a rapidly changing youth and family culture. You are fine young men. I cherish my days walking by your side and I cheer you on as you travel far beyond where I can go.

I'm thankful for the investment that the Awana tribe has made in me, and grateful to be a part of such a growing team of kidmin leaders. Proud to serve alongside of you and must say "thank you" to: Brian, Colin, Valerie, Gary, Steve, Ken, Cindy, Michael S., Jeremy, Mike L., Zac, Bunker, Mike H., Dan, Donna, Jon, Charles, Gajendra, Runar, AnneLene, Tom, Ed, Mike R., Arlyn, and so many others.

And to the leaders who have walked beside me by investing their spiritual legacy and leadership wisdom into me, I thank: Ron, Steve, Sean, Dean, Rob, Mark, Mom, Mike W., Mike A., Sherry, Jerry, Michael W., Katie G., Tom, Eddie, Michael L., Jeff, Tommy, Heath, Randy, Chris and numerous others.

Pat, you are a true champion. Your heart for Jesus as your friend, redeemer, and king shines so brightly. It's difficult for you to breath without giving glory or declaring dependence upon Christ. You embody the characteristics of being a beloved child of God.

We'd both like to thank Duane, Betsey, Parker, and the Moody Publishers team for believing in us and providing this opportunity. Your insights are incredible. You provided excellent support and advice and helped us shape our thoughts for Christ and His glory.

Lastly, we thank Kidmin Leaders who allowed us to share their stories in this book. You have made this book complete.

About the Authors

Pat Cimo:

For nearly twenty-nine years, Pat has led a dynamic children's ministry and coached children's ministry leaders domestically and internationally. She is currently the Director of Marriage and Family Life at Willow Creek Community Church. As a director and a church-wide leadership team member, Pat has many opportunities to lead change within the local church. She has a deep passion for influencing and developing champions of faith.

Pat and her husband, Dave, live in the northwest suburbs of Chicago near their two married children and four grandchildren. Her favorite days of the week are Monday and Friday when she becomes known for her favorite role—"Nonni" to grandchildren Jenna, Taryn, David, and Ellie.

Matt Markins:

Matt serves on the Global Leadership Team at Awana as the Vice President of Ministry Resources, as well as the Vice President of Marketing and Strategy. Prior to joining the Awana executive leadership team, Matt served in leadership roles with Thomas Nelson Publishers and Randall House Publishers, and was the cofounder of the D6 Conference (a discipleship and family ministry community).

Matt's ministry in organizational leadership has been marked by leading and influencing change from within by casting vision, forging strategic partnerships, nurturing healthy culture, developing organizational alignment, and implementing sustainable plans toward ministry effectiveness, health and growth. He and his wife, Katie, have been volunteering and growing in children's ministry for more than twenty years. As Nashville transplants, they live and play in the Chicago suburbs with their two sons, tolerating dreadful winters but soaking up refreshingly mild weather the other seven months of the year.

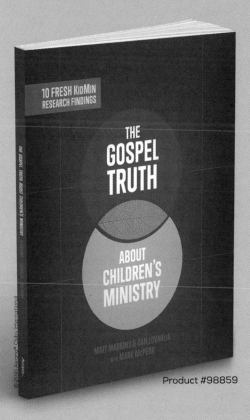

ONCE I TRULY UNDERSTOOD THE *beauty of Awana*

I KNEW THAT OUR CHURCH NEEDED TO EMBRACE IT.

it's the BEST DISCIPLE-SHIP *program out there.*

Pat Cimo, Director of Family Life
WILLOW CREEK COMMUNITY CHURCH

MOODY
Radio™

*From the Word **to Life***

Moody Radio produces and delivers compelling programs filled with biblical insights and creative expressions of faith that help you take the next step in your relationship with Christ.

You can hear Moody Radio on 36 stations and more than 1,500 radio outlets across the U.S. and Canada. Or listen on your smartphone with the Moody Radio app!

www.moodyradio.org